THE HEALTH INSURANCE PORTABILITY AND ACCOUNTABILITY ACT (HIPAA):
OVERVIEW AND ANALYSES

THE HEALTH INSURANCE PORTABILITY AND ACCOUNTABILITY ACT (HIPAA):
OVERVIEW AND ANALYSES

HINDA R. CHAIKIND, JEAN HEARNE, BOB LYKE,
C. STEPHEN REDHEAD, JULIE STONE,
CELINDA FRANCO AND GINA MARIE STEVENS

Novinka Books
New York

Senior Editors: Susan Boriotti and Donna Dennis
Coordinating Editor: Tatiana Shohov
Office Manager: Annette Hellinger
Graphics: Wanda Serrano and Matt Dallow
Editorial Production: Maya Columbus, Alexis Klestov, Vladimir Klestov,
    Matthew Kozlowski and Lorna Loperfido
Circulation: Ave Maria Gonzalez, Vera Popovic, Luis Aviles, Sean Corkery,
    Raymond Davis, Melissa Diaz, Meagan Flaherty, Magdalena Nuñez,
    Marlene Nuñez, Jeannie Pappas and Frankie Punger
Communications and Acquisitions: Serge P. Shohov
Marketing: Cathy DeGregory

Library of Congress Cataloging-in-Publication Data
The Health Insurance Portability and Accountability Act (HIPAA): overview and analysis / H.R. Chaikind ... [et al.].
    p. cm.
Includes index.
    ISBN 1-59033-904-5.

1. Medical records-Law and legislation-United States. 2. Medical records-Access control-United States. 3. United States. Health Insurance Portability and Accountability Act of 1996.
    [DNLM: 1. United States. Health Insurance Portability and Accountability Act of 1996. 2. Insurance, Health-legislation & jurisprudence-United States. 3. Confidentiality-legislation & jurisprudence-United States. 4. Medical Records-legislation & jurisprudence-United States. 5. Privacy-legislation & jurisprudence-United States. W 32.5 AA1 H4343 2003] I. Chaikind, H. R.

KF3827.R4 H33 2003
344.7304'1-dc22   2003024205

Copyright © 2004 by Novinka Books, An Imprint of
    Nova Science Publishers, Inc.
    400 Oser Ave, Suite 1600
    Hauppauge, New York 11788-3619
    Tele. 631-231-7269   Fax 631-231-8175
    e-mail: Novascience@earthlink.net
    Web Site: http://www.novapublishers.com

All rights reserved. No part of this book may be reproduced, stored in a retrieval system or transmitted in any form or by any means: electronic, electrostatic, magnetic, tape, mechanical photocopying, recording or otherwise without permission from the publishers.

The publisher has taken reasonable care in the preparation of this book, but makes no expressed or implied warranty of any kind and assumes no responsibility for any errors or omissions. No liability is assumed for incidental or consequential damages in connection with or arising out of information contained in this book. Any parts of this book based on government reports are so indicated and copyright is claimed for those parts to the extent applicable to compilations of such works.

This publication is designed to provide accurate and authoritative information with regard to the subject matter covered herein. It is sold with the clear understanding that the publisher is not engaged in rendering legal or any other professional services. If legal or any other expert assistance is required, the services of a competent person should be sought. FROM A DECLARATION OF PARTICIPANTS JOINTLY ADOPTED BY A COMMITTEE OF THE AMERICAN BAR ASSOCIATION AND A COMMITTEE OF PUBLISHERS.

Printed in the United States of America

CONTENTS

Preface		vii
Chapter 1	The Health Insurance Portability and Accountability Act (HIPAA): Summary of the Administrative Simplification Provisions *Celinda Franco*	1
Chapter 2	The Health Insurance Portability and Accountability Act (HIPAA): Overview and Guidance on Frequently Asked Questions *Hinda R. Chaikind, Jean Hearne, Bob Lyke, C. Stephen Redhead and Julie Stone*	19
Chapter 3	Health Information Standards, Privacy, and Security: HIPAA's Administrative Simplification Regulations *C. Stephen Redhead*	53
Chapter 4	A Brief Summary of the HIPAA Medical Privacy Rule *Gina Marie Stevens*	91
Chapter 5	Medical Records Privacy: Questions and Answers on the HIPAA Final Rule *C. Stephen Redhead*	101
Chapter 6	Compliance with the HIPAA Medical Privacy Rule *Gina Marie Stevens*	109
Index		117

PREFACE

The Health Insurance Portability and Accountability Act (HIPAA) of 1996 (P.L. 104-191) mandates significant changes in the health insurance industry, and includes as a small part of the overall insurance reforms, requirements for the standardization of electronically transmitted health insurance financial claims and administrative transactions. Congress enacted a provision which prohibits federally appropriated funds from being used to adopt a final standard providing for a unique health identifier for an individual until legislation is enacted specifically approving the standard. Chapter one summarizes the Act and the issues.

The Health Insurance Portability and Accountability Act (HIPAA) of 1996 (P.L. 104-191) continues to generate numerous questions. What kinds of policies does it cover? Does it help people who are currently uninsured? Does it help people with preexisting medical conditions? How does it affect health insurance premiums? How do its requirements interact with the Consolidated Omnibus Budget Reconciliation Act (COBRA) continuation coverage? Answers to those questions, as well as other commonly asked questions, are provided in chapter two, as well as descriptions of each of the major section of HIPAA.

The Administrative Simplification provisions of the Health Insurance Portability and Accountability Act of 1996 (HIPAA, P.L. 104-191, 42 U.S.C. 1320d) instructed the Secretary of Health and Human Services (HHS) to develop standards to support electronic data interchange for a variety of administrative and financial health care transactions. The intent of the legislation is to improve health care system efficiency and effectiveness, make it easier to detect fraud and abuse, facilitate access to health and medical information by researchers, and reduce administrative costs. The third chapter is divided into two sections. The first provides some background on electronic health information security and privacy. The second includes summaries of the various proposed HIPAA standards and the status of their implementation. Particular attention is given to the provisions of the proposed privacy standards and the public comments HHS has received on this proposal.

Chapter four provides an overview of the final rule for "Standards for the Privacy of Individually Identifiable Health Information" ("privacy rule") that was issued by the Department of Health and Human Services (DHHS) and went into effect on April 14, 2001. Entities covered by the privacy rule had until April 2003 to comply, with the exception of small health plans who have until 2004.

On December 28, 2000, the Secretary of Health and Human Services issued a final regulation (65 Fed. Reg. 82462) to protect the privacy of personally identifiable health information maintained or transmitted in electronic form. The regulations do not preempt, or override, state laws that are more protective of medical records privacy. Chapter five talks about these issues and gives answers to the most pertinent questions.

As of April 14, 2003, most health care providers (including doctors and hospitals) and health plans are required to comply with the new Privacy Rule mandated by the Health Insurance Portability and Accountability Act of 1996 (HIPAA), and must comply with national standards to protect individually identifiable health information. On April 17, 2003, HHS published an interim final rule establishing the rules of procedure for investigations and the imposition of civil money penalties concerning violations. Chapter six highlights these issues.

Chapter 1

THE HEALTH INSURANCE PORTABILITY AND ACCOUNTABILITY ACT (HIPAA): SUMMARY OF THE ADMINISTRATIVE SIMPLIFICATION PROVISIONS[*]

Celinda Franco

ADMINISTRATIVE SIMPLIFICATION

Background

Each year the health care industry generates billions of financial and administrative transactions in both paper and electronic form that result from the delivery of health care services. Seeking ways to lower the costs of delivering health care, health care payers and providers have long sought ways to simplify the administration of health care financial transactions. Over the years, many in the health care industry looked to electronic information systems and various computer technologies as potential tools for achieving the administrative simplification of health care transactions. Despite attempts to develop standards for the uniform processing of health care claims and related administrative transactions electronically, payers and

---

[*] Excerpted from CRS Report 98-964 EPW.

providers failed to reach agreement on the standardization of these transactions.

Currently, there are no standardized formats for the electronic or paper transmission of health care information, or standards for identifying providers, health plans, employers or individuals participating in the health care system. There are approximately 400 formats for electronic health claims used in the United States today. The absence of standardized formats for health claims means that payers and providers must frequently invest in multiple computer systems or programs, as well as additional human resources in order to process claims with different format requirements. This increases the administrative costs of health care delivery. The lack of standardization limits the efficient flow of information between payers and providers, increases the complexity and costs of processing of health care claims and other financial and administrative transactions, and hinders efforts to detect fraud and abuse.

Today health care information is used for many purposes by a variety of individuals and organizations within and outside the health care industry. Primary users of health care information include physicians, clinics, and hospitals that provide care to patients. Patients provide health care information to their physicians to supply historical background so their health care needs can be assessed. Physicians use this information to develop appropriate treatment plans, order diagnostic tests, and maintain an ongoing medical record of services provided to a patient. Hospitals and clinics use health care information to provide patient care ordered by physicians and maintain ongoing records of health care services provided. To receive payment for health care services, providers must bill either patients or health insurers for reimbursement. In order for providers to be reimbursed by health insurers, provider claims often must include certain information about the patient's medical records to justify that the services provided were appropriate. Insurance claims often include such patient-specific information as diagnosis, treatment, and prognosis.

Secondary users of health care information include organizations that pay for health care benefits, such as traditional health insurance companies, managed care providers, and government programs, like Medicare and Medicaid. As a part of their management functions, these health care payers also use health care information to analyze the cost and quality of health care delivered by various providers. Other secondary users of health information include medical and social science researchers, employers, and public health services, for purposes such as researching the costs and benefits of alternative medical treatments, determining eligibility for social programs, and understanding state and local health care needs. Much of the health care data that is available to secondary users specifically identifies individuals, and may or may not have required the patient's consent to grant access to some secondary users.

The transformation of the health care industry by the expansion of managed care and other integrated delivery systems, has further increased the amount of health care information that is routinely being exchanged between insurers and providers as they seek to inform coverage and payment decisions with health care data. Much of the data being exchanged contains patient-identifiable information about private, often sensitive, health care matters. In the absence of uniform laws protecting the privacy rights of patients, the increased dissemination of health data raises serious concerns about the privacy and security of health care information. This is a particularly important concern when health care information is transmitted electronically and there may not be adequate security measures in place to protect unauthorized access to patient-identifiable data and misuse of such information.

The Health Insurance Portability and Accountability Act of 1996 (HIPAA, P.L. 104-191, 42 USC §1320d) enacted on August 21, 1996, added a new Part C — Administrative Simplification — to Title XI of the Social Security Act. HIPAA established requirements and standards for the electronic transmission of health information that are intended to improve health care system efficiency and effectiveness, make it easier to detect fraud and abuse, facilitate access to health and medical information by researchers, and reduce administrative costs. Under HIPAA, health information is defined as any information, whether oral or recorded in any form or medium that is created or received by a health care provider, health plan, public health authority, employer, life insurer, school or university, or health care clearinghouse. Health information can relate to the past, present, or future physical or mental health or condition of an individual, the provision of health care to an individual, or the past, present, or future payment for the provision of health care to an individual. HIPAA does not, however, provide for the collection of clinical data or the electronic maintenance of patient medical records. As such, HIPAA's overarching goal in this area is to serve as a catalyst for the health care industry to increasingly use electronic transactions and standard formats so that significant administrative savings can be achieved.

General Requirements for Adoption of Standards

HIPAA requires the Secretary of the Department of Health and Human Services (HHS) to adopt standards for the financial and administrative transactions used in the operation of the health care system to enable health information to be exchanged electronically. The standards mandated by HIPAA apply to all health plans, health care clearinghouses, and health care providers that transmit health information electronically.[1] The standards are required to reduce the administrative costs of providing and paying for health care. Any standard adopted by the Secretary must have been developed, adopted, or modified by standard setting organizations.[2] The Secretary may adopt a different standard if the different standard will substantially reduce administrative costs to health care providers, and the standard is promulgated in accordance with federal rulemaking procedures. If no standard has been adopted by any standard setting organization that is required by HIPAA, the Secretary is required to rely on the recommendations of the National Committee on Vital and Health Statistics (NCVHS) and consult with the standard setting organizations, appropriate federal and state agencies, and private organizations. In general, for any standard adopted by the Secretary, the law further specifies that the following organizations must be consulted: the National Uniform Billing Committee, the National Uniform Claim Committee, the Workgroup for Electronic Data Interchange, and the American Dental Association.

---

[1] HIPAA defines a *health plan* to include individual or group plans that provide, or pay the cost of, medical care, including group health plans, health insurance issuers, health maintenance organizations, Medicare, Medicaid, a long-term care policy, an employee welfare benefit plan or other arrangement covering employees of two or more employers, military health care programs, the Veterans health care program, the Civilian Health and Medical Program of the Uniformed Services (CHAMPUS), the Indian Health Service program, and the Federal Employees Health Benefit Program. HIPAA defines a *health care clearinghouse* as a public or private entity that processes or facilitates the processing of nonstandard data elements of health information into standard data elements. HIPAA defines a *health care provider* to include a provider of medical or other health services, or any other person furnishing health care services or supplies.

[2] The law defines a standard setting organization as an organization accredited by the American National Standards Institute, including the National Council for Prescription Drug Programs, that develops standards for information transactions data elements, or any other standard that is necessary to, or will facilitate, the implementation of the administrative simplification provisions in HIPAA.

Standards for Information Transactions and Data Elements

HIPAA establishes general requirements for standards for electronic transactions adopted by the Secretary. These include standards for:

- **Transactions to allow the electronic exchange of health information,** such as health claims and attachments, health plan enrollment and disenrollment, health plan eligibility, health care payment and remittance advice, premium payments, first report of injury, claim status, and referral certification and authorization.

- **Unique identifiers** for individuals, employers, health plans, and health care providers, with the authorized uses identified.

- **Code sets for data elements for standard transactions** using established sets of codes for data elements such as tables of terms, medical concepts, medical diagnostic codes, or medical procedure codes.

- **Security standards** for entities that maintain or transmit health information in order to provide "reasonable and appropriate" administrative, technical, and physical safeguards for confidentiality and security of the information,

- **Electronic signatures** specifying procedures for the electronic transmission and authentication of signatures.

- **Transfer of information among health plans** for the coordination of benefits, sequential claims processing, and other data elements for individuals with more than one health plan.

Timetables for Adoption of Standards[3]

HIPAA provides timetables for the Secretary, in consultation with standard-setting organizations and providers, to develop and adopt standards for electronic transactions. HHS is required to **develop** the standards for *electronic transactions* by February 21, 1998, and **adopt** standards by August 21, 1998. The standards for *claims attachments* are required by February 21, 1999.

---

[3] For more information about implementation deadlines established in HIPAA, see Appendix A at the end of the report.

HHS issued a proposed rule in the *Federal Register* (v. 63, no. 88, p. 25272) on May 7, 1998, for the standards for electronic transactions and code sets, and the requirements for implementing these standards. The proposed rule would establish the requirements that health plans, health care clearinghouses, and certain health care providers would have to meet. Proposed rules were also issued for the identifier for employers on June 6, 1998 (v. 63, no. 115, p. 32784), and for security standards on August 12, 1998 (v. 63, no. 155, p. 43242).

Requirements for Conducting Transactions

Health plans are required to process a transaction electronically that is submitted electronically, in a standard format, and may not delay or adversely affect transactions submitted electronically. Information that is submitted and received electronically is required to be in standard data elements. Plans can meet the requirements to transmit and receive such data either directly or by contracting with a health care clearinghouse to convert nonstandard data elements into standard transactions. After the final rules are issued by HHS, health plans or persons to whom the standards apply have 2 years to comply, and small health plans[4] have 3 years. A plan or person may comply voluntarily before the effective date of the standards, and may comply by using a health care clearinghouse to transmit or receive the standard transactions. If a standard is modified, compliance with the modified standard may not be earlier than 180 days after notice of the change.

HIPAA does *not* require providers and payers to electronically transmit claims and related transactions. However, if they transmit or accept transactions electronically, they must be submitted in the standard format adopted by the Secretary.

General Penalty for Failure to Comply with Standards

HIPAA establishes a $100 civil monetary penalty per person per violation, and not more than $25,000 in a calendar year per person per violation of a single standard. The procedural provisions of Section 1128A

---

[4] HCFA proposed in the *Federal Register* on May 7, 1998, that small health plans be defined as plans with 50 or fewer participants.

of the Social Security Act apply.[5] There are limitations on when a penalty may be imposed, including instances where the failure to comply with the standards was due to offenses otherwise punishable (described separately, below), or where the person liable for the penalty did not know, and would not have known that the provision had been violated exercising reasonable diligence. In addition, the penalty may not be imposed if the failure to comply was due to reasonable cause and not willful neglect, and was corrected within 30 days of learning that the Mure to comply had occurred. The Secretary is given discretion to extend the 30-day correction period, and is permitted to provide technical assistance in certain cases. In cases where the failure to comply was due to reasonable cause and not to willful neglect, the penalty may be waived.

Wrongful Disclosure of Individually Identifiable Health Information

Recognizing the vulnerable nature of information transmitted electronically, HIPAA establishes penalties for knowing misuse of unique health identifiers and individually identifiable health information. The penalties for wrongfully obtaining or disclosing individually identifiable information are: (1) a fine of up to $50,000 and/or imprisonment of not more than one year, (2) if committed under false pretenses, a fine of not more than $100,000, imprisonment of not more than 5 years, or both; and (3) if the offense is committed with intent to sell, transfer, or use individually identifiable information for commercial advantage, personal gain, or to do "malicious harm," a fine of up to $250,000, imprisonment of not more than 10 years, or both.

Effect on State Law

The standards adopted or modified under HIPAA shall supersede contrary provisions in state law pertaining to health information, including provisions of state law requiring medical records to be maintained in written rather than electronic form. State laws on health information include statutes governing the use and disclosure of such information, inspection and copying of health information, procedures for correction and amendment of

---

[5] Section 1128A provides for civil and monetary penalty provisions under Medicare and Medicaid programs.

health information, and maintenance requirements for health information and medical records.[6] The HIPAA standards do not supersede provisions in state law to detect fraud and abuse, to regulate insurance and health plans, for reporting health care delivery or costs, or for regulation of controlled substances. Moreover, HIPAA's requirements cannot be construed to invalidate or limit state laws requiring the reporting of disease, injury, child abuse, birth or death, public health surveillance, or public health investigation or intervention. States may continue to require reporting of health information for management and financial audits, program monitoring and evaluation, and licensure or certification.

Processing Payment Transactions by Financial Institutions

HIPAA standards do not apply to the activities of financial institutions related to authorizing, processing, clearing, settling, billing, transferring, reconciling, or collecting payments for a financial institution. The conference report explains that Congress intended that the law would not apply to the use or disclosure of information when an individual utilized a payment system to make a payment for, or related to, health plan premiums or health care. As an example, the conference report describes a situation where the standards of HIPAA would not apply when the exchange of information between participants in a credit card system is made in connection with processing a credit card payment for health care. Another example given of a situation not covered by HIPAA's requirements would be when a financial institution sends a checking account statement to an account holder who uses a credit or debit card to pay for health care services. However, if such a company clears health care claims, then the health care claims activities of the company would be subject to HIPAA requirements.

---

[6] For a further discussion of the complexities of preempting existing state laws, see *Confidentiality of Individually-Identifiable Health Information, Recommendations of the Secretary of Health and Human Services, Pursuant to Section 264 of the Health Insurance Portability and Accountability Act of* 1996, September 11, 1997 (available on the Internet at [http://aspe.os.dhhs.gov/admnsimp/pvcrec0.htm]).

Changes in Membership and Duties of National Committee on Vital and Health Statistics

HIPAA amends the Public Health Service Act to increase the membership of the NCVHS from 16 to 18 members and requires the Committee to assist and advise the Secretary on issues related to statistical problems bearing on health and health services that are of national and international interest. HIPAA required the NCVHS to report to Congress by August 1997 on the implementation of the standards and requirements provided by the law. The NCVHS submitted this report in July 1997 (available on the Internet at [http://aspe.os.dhhs.gov/ncvhs/reptrecs.htm]). The NCVHS is also required to study the issues related to the adoption of uniform data standards for patient medical record information and the electronic exchange of this information, and report to Congress 4 years after the date of HIPAA's enactment (August 2000).

HHS RECOMMENDATIONS WITH RESPECT TO PRIVACY OF CERTAIN HEALTH INFORMATION

HIPAA required HHS to submit by August 1997, a report with recommendations on federal standards for protecting the privacy of individually identifiable health information to the Senate Labor and Human Resources and Finance Committees and the House Ways and Means Committee. The recommendations for privacy standards were required to address the privacy rights of individuals, procedures to exercise those rights, and uses and disclosure of the information that should be authorized or required under the law. The law established a timetable requiring the Congress to enact legislation to address the privacy issue within 36 months of enactment (August 21, 1999). If the Congress fails to act by that date, the Secretary would then be required by the law to issue privacy protections through final regulation within 42 months of HIPAA enactment (February 21, 2000). These privacy regulations could be preempted by more stringent state law.

The Secretary of HHS submitted the Department's report to Congress on September 11, 1997, at a hearing before the Senate Committee on Labor and Human Resources. The recommendations include five key principles that the Secretary argues must form the foundation for legislation to guarantee the privacy of individually identifiable health information. These principles are:

- Limit, with few exceptions, the use of an individual's health care information to health purposes only;

- Require organizations that are entrusted with health information (including providers and payers, service organizations, organizations receiving information for specified purposes without patient authorization, organizations receiving information with a patient's authorization, and employers) to provide adequate security measures to protect that information from misuse or disclosure;

- Provide patients with new rights to control how their health information is used, such as the ability to get copies of records and propose corrections;

- Hold those who misuse personal health information accountable and provide redress for persons harmed by its misuse through criminal and civil penalties, and

- Balance privacy protections with public responsibility to support national priorities including public health, research, quality care, and reduction of fraud and abuse, including allowing law enforcement access to personal health information within existing law.

Under the HHS recommendations, "health care information" would be defined to include medical records held in any form. The recommendations apply to health care providers and payers, as well as to entities that receive information from providers and payers (vendors or clearinghouses that handle the information). The HHS report also recommended that the sale of patient lists by medical service organizations be made illegal. In addition, HHS recommends that individually identifiable health information should be available without the patient's consent to public health authorities for disease reporting, public health investigation, or intervention, and in certain cases of medical research. Health care information would be considered "identifiable" if there is a reasonable basis to believe that it can be used to identity an individual.

The report recommended that insurers or health care professionals be required to give patients a written explanation detailing who has access to their information; how that information was kept; how they could restrict or limit access to it; how they could authorize disclosure or revoke such authorization; and what their rights would be should an improper disclosure occur. The HHS report also recommended a process for patients to seek corrections or amendments to their health information.

The report recommended that existing confidentiality laws at both state and federal levels which provide more protection remain in force and not be superseded by any new federal legislation. The recommendation concluded that a new federal privacy law should provide a basic level of protection, or "floor" of protection, without preempting more stringent existing laws. Critics of this recommendation argue that there needs to be federal standardization of privacy law because of the lack of uniformity among state laws, and without preemption individuals in states with weak or no privacy protections in place are disadvantaged. Opponents of preemption argue that stricter laws in some states could be lost with a uniform federal law, and therefore state laws should be left in place.

The HHS report also recommended that current state laws that permit disclosure to law enforcement officials for legitimate law enforcement purposes not be changed or limited by federal privacy law. This would include disclosure of medical information, without patient consent, to law enforcement officials for purposes required by state law, such as reporting gunshot wound victims, identification or location of an injured fugitive, or for other "legitimate" law enforcement purposes. This recommendation has been particularly contentious among privacy advocates, who have asserted that law enforcement officials should be required to obtain a judicial warrant or subpoena to gain access to medical records.

The HHS report recommended that individuals or organizations should be subject to criminal felony penalties (including fines and imprisonment) if they knowingly obtain or use health care information without authorization. The penalties would be higher when violations are for monetary gain. Civil monetary penalties would apply when there is a demonstrated pattern or practice of unauthorized disclosure. Persons whose privacy rights were violated would be able to sue for damages and equitable relief and could obtain attorney's fees and punitive damages if the violation was done knowingly.

While the HHS recommendations were generally regarded as a step in the right direction for establishing minimum federal protections for individually identifiable health information, critics argued that serious concerns remained unresolved.

ISSUES

Unique Health Identifier for Individuals

According to HHS, the unique identifier for individuals is an essential component of the administrative simplification provisions enacted in HIPAA.[7] HHS contends that the ability to identity individuals in the health system would have benefits, including improved quality of care and reduced administrative costs and that unique individual health information is also essential in the delivery of health care. Currently, many types of health care organizations and insurance companies, integrated delivery systems, health plans, managed care organizations, public programs, clinics, hospitals, physicians, and pharmacies routinely assign individuals identifiers for use within their systems. On the other hand, concerns are emerging about the potential uses and abuses of a unique health identifier for individuals.

The HIPAA law requires the Secretary, in consultation with the NCVHS, to adopt unique identifiers for individuals, health care providers, health plans, and employers. The law requires that standards for transactions, the unique health identifier for individuals being one of those, be proposed by February 21, 1998. The law also requires the Secretary to establish specific purposes for which a unique health identifier can be used. The development of a standard unique identifier for individuals required under HIPAA has sparked privacy and confidentiality concerns.

The most obvious advantage of a unique individual identifier is that it might contribute to simplification of the health system and potentially reduced costs for institutions and reimbursement systems. Individual identifiers could assist researchers in conducting longitudinal studies, as well as facilitate the linkage of valuable health data about a patient that might be useful in providing improved health care delivery. At the same time, individual identifiers raise serious privacy concerns. Opponents of using an individual identifier argue that, depending on which number were selected as the individual identifier, the use of such a number could increase the ease of linking medical records with other records about an individual, such as financial data or employment information. Some raise the concern that individual identifiers could facilitate access to personal information by unscrupulous employers or insurers who could then use that information to discriminate in hiring or insuring individuals with serious or costly health

---

[7] For more information, see HHS White paper available via the Internet at |lbttp://aspe.os.dhhs. gov/admnsimp/nprm/noiwpl.htm].

problems, or in some way harm the interests of the individual. Some providers have even argued that concerns about the vulnerability of individually identifiable information may keep some individuals from fully disclosing their health problems to their health care providers.

Some privacy advocates believe that standardized patient identifiers should not be employed under any circumstances. Others maintain that, if any identifiers are deemed valuable, they need to be accompanied by strict policy guidance on appropriate use, allowable linkages among records, adequate auditing capability, and appropriate sanctions for misuse.

While there has been considerable consensus on most of the standards required by HIPAA, HHS acknowledges that opinion on the unique identifier for individuals is deeply divided. In an attempt to address the controversy surrounding the use of an individual identifier, HHS has departed from the customary rulemaking process and is holding a series of regional hearings to examine the privacy concerns. The first of these hearings was held in Chicago on July 20-21, 1998. After the remaining hearings are completed and the public comments are assimilated, HHS plans to issue a proposed rule followed by a public comment period. Once HHS considers and responds to comments, it will then publish a final rule to implement a unique health identifier for individuals. The Congress then has 60 days to consider the final rule, and either let it go into effect or disapprove it.

The first regional hearing in Chicago sparked such controversy that on July 31, 1998, the Administration announced its intention to delay the implementation of a unique health identifier for individuals until privacy legislation is enacted.[8] The delay would give officials more time to examine the impact of a unique health identifier.

In response to the concerns about the unique patient identifier, two bills were introduced in the 105th Congress to repeal the requirement for HHS to adopt a standard unique patient identifier under HIPAA. On July 22, 1998, Representative Barr introduced HR. 4312, the *Medical Privacy Protection Act of 1998.* H.R. 4312 would have repealed section 1173(b) of the Social Security Act, which requires the Secretary to adopt standards for unique identifiers for individuals, employers, health plans, and health care providers. The bin would also have prohibited federal agencies from issuing, using, or establishing a national medical identification card, or directing a state to issue or modify an identification card or document in order to satisfy

---

[8] Brinkley, Joel. Gore Outlines Privacy Measures, but Their Impact Is Small. *The New York Times,* August 1, 1998. [http://www.nytimes.com/library/tech/98/08/biztech/articles/o1health-numbers-side.html]

any federal requirement. On July 24, 1998, a similar bill, S. 2352, the *Patient Privacy Rights Act of 1998,* was introduced by Senator Leahy. These bills died in committee without hearings. The Omnibus Consolidated and Emergency Supplemental Appropriations for FY1999, H.R. 4328 (P.L. 105-277), provided that no funds be used to adopt a final standard providing for a unique health identifier for an individual until legislation is enacted specifically approving the standard.

Privacy Legislation in the 105th Congress

The privacy and confidentiality of health information is an important public policy concern. At the federal level, although health information is protected under several different laws, there is no comprehensive federal medical privacy law. State laws generally define the types of health information considered confidential and the circumstances under which health information can be disclosed. However, existing laws provide a patchwork of protections that are often limited in scope.

Many in Congress have long been concerned with the need to protect the confidentiality and privacy of health information, and privacy legislation has been introduced for a number of years. However, the requirements of the administrative simplification provisions of HIPAA provide greater incentive to consider protections for individually identifiable health information. If the Congress fails to enact privacy legislation by August 1999, the Secretary must promulgate such protections through the regulatory process by February 2000.

Privacy protections for individually identifiable health information is at the center of the implementation of the HIPAA law on administrative simplification. While HIPAA requires that entities receiving health information establish security standards that take "real and reasonable" steps to safeguard that information, federal privacy legislation is seen by many as necessary to set a uniform, basic level of protections for health information. While there is broad agreement on the underlying principles of privacy from most of the health care industry, there was no consensus reached on many significant aspects of the privacy bills introduced in the 105th Congress.[9] Six bills were introduced to address medical records privacy in the 105th

---

[9] For a more complete discussion of the legislation, see CRS Issue Brief 98002, *Medical Records Confidentiality,* by Irene Stith-Coleman, Coordinator.

Congress. In addition, 10 other bills were introduced specifically on protecting the privacy of genetic information.[10]

The six bills that were introduced on the general topic of medical records privacy are HR. 52 (Condit), H.R 1815 (McDermott), H.R. 3900 (Shays), S. 1368 (Leahy), S. 1921 (Jeffords), and S.2609 (Bennett). Generally, these bills would have placed restrictions on use and disclosure of personalty-identifiable health information, established security and auditing capabilities for records systems, ensured patient access to their records, provided the right to seek corrections, required entities to provide notices of their privacy practices, and established penalties for abuse of privacy rights. The bills varied on how privacy protections would be assured, in what way federal law would have preempted state laws, to what degree use of informed consent or federal statutes would have served as the basis for allowable disclosures, and what specific safeguards would have been implemented to protect individuals when non-consensual disclosures would be permitted. A number of hearings were held on these proposals; however, none of the bills were enacted in the 105th Congress.

Privacy provisions for health information were also included in much broader legislation designed to regulate health insurance provided through managed care plans, as discussed above.[11] H.R. 3605 and S. 1890/S. 1891, *the Patients' Bill of Rights Act of 1998,* H.R. 4250, the *Patient Protection Act of 1998,* as passed by the House on July 24, 1998, and S. 2330, the *Patient's Bill of Rights Act,* introduced on July 17, 1998, were some of the bills which included provisions designed to protect the confidentiality of health information. All of the bills would have required health insurance plans to allow individuals to inspect and copy protected health information, and H.R. 4250 and S. 2330 would also have allowed patients to amend their protected health information. The bills would have required health care providers and other entities (including law enforcement officials as in S.2330) to post or provide a notice of confidentiality practices, and required insurers to establish safeguards to protect the privacy of individually identifiable information. H.R. 4250 would have allowed any person who maintains protected health information to disclose it to a health care provider or a health plan in order for a provider or plan to conduct health care operations, but would have prohibited a provider or plan from selling or bartering

---

[10] For more information on genetic discrimination, see CRS Report 97-873, *Genetic Discrimination Legislation in the 105th Congress: A Bill Comparison,* by Irene Stith-Coleman and Angela Choy.

[11] For a side-by side comparison of the provisions of these bills, see CRS Report 98-643, *Side-by-Side Comparison of Selected Patient Protection Bills: H.R. 4250, H.R. 3605, S. 1890/S. 1891, and S. 2330,* by Jason Lee, Coordinator.

protected health information as a part of conducting health care operations. Only H.R. 4250 would have explicitly required federal preemption of certain state laws related to protected health information. All of the bills would have imposed civil penalties for failure to comply with the confidentiality provisions of the bills. H.R. 4250 was passed by the House on July 24, 1998, however the bill was not considered in the Senate even though the bill was placed on the Senate calendar.

There is general consensus among the health care industry that a federal statute that provides baseline medical records privacy protection is necessary and would generally improve safeguards for health information that currently are provided through the existing patchwork of state and federal laws. There also is strong support for a legislative solution to this issue, rather than relying on federal regulations to protect health privacy rights. Yet there is little agreement on many of the specific privacy provisions of the bills that were introduced during the 105th Congress.

The most frequently raised objections to the privacy legislation introduced in the 105th Congress tended to include the following three major legal issues: patient rights to access and amend medical records, limits on law enforcement access, and preemption of existing state laws. Patient rights advocates argued that patients should be informed about information maintained about them, be allowed to amend or supplement their records, and give their consent about disclosures of their information. Provider groups, while recognizing the need to protect individual privacy rights, argued that the right to see and amend medical records, as well as informed consent requirements for disclosure, would make their compliance burdensome. Some states currently have laws that protect a patient's right to informed consent and limit allowable disclosures without patient consent. In some states disclosure limits on patient information are only provided for certain medical conditions or illnesses, such as AIDS or mental health. However, in many states there are no laws protecting health information disclosures.

The second prominent issue in the debate relates to the need to balance patient control over disclosures of health information with the need for appropriate exemptions from informed patient consent, such as instances where law enforcement officials would need to have access to patient records for evidence of illegal activity. Privacy advocates argue that law enforcement access should not be expanded to allow wider or unlimited access to patient information. Law enforcement officials argue that restricting access to medical records hampers their ability to conduct investigations and collect evidence for criminal prosecutions. In some states law enforcement officials are required to obtain search warrants to have access to medical records, while in most states there are no laws limiting disclosures of health information.

A third contentious issue in the privacy debate is about overriding existing state laws, or preemption. Industry advocates argue that having to comply with varying requirements for health information and medical records in different states is burdensome, and a federal law is needed to standardize these requirements by preempting state law. Privacy advocates argue that in some states existing laws provide greater protections for individually identifiable health information and should not be superseded by federal law. While most health industry advocates agree that a federal law is needed to provide a standard or "floor" of protection, there is no consensus about whether or not federal law should preempt existing state privacy laws.

CONCLUSION

HIPAA's requirements for administrative simplification were generally welcomed by the health industry after years of failing to agree on standards that would achieve uniformity in financial and administrative transactions. Among the participants in the health industry there has largely been agreement on the standards and requirements being implemented by HIPAA. However, two extremely contentious issues have surfaced and are inextricably linked together in a way that may slow the implementation of the law: the unique individual identifier and the need for federal privacy protections in a standardized and integrated health industry. If legislation to eliminate the HIPAA requirement for a unique individual identifier (as well as the employer, health plan and provider identifiers) is enacted, it may prove difficult to achieve the administrative simplification desired by some. Moreover, the privacy debate has ensued for years with little consensus on the best approach for federal legislation. If the implementation of the unique individual health identifier is delayed until federal privacy protections are in place, then the full implementation of HIPAA's administrative simplification provisions may also be delayed.

Chapter 2

THE HEALTH INSURANCE PORTABILITY AND ACCOUNTABILITY ACT (HIPAA): OVERVIEW AND GUIDANCE ON FREQUENTLY ASKED QUESTIONS[+]

Hinda R. Chaikind, Jean Hearne, Bob Lyke, C. Stephen Redhead and Julie Stone

The Health Insurance Portability and Accountability Act of 1996 (P.L. 104-191, HIPAA) provided for changes in the health insurance market and imposed certain federal requirements on health insurance plans offered by public and private employers. It guaranteed the availability and renewability of health insurance coverage for certain employees and individuals, and limited the use of preexisting condition restrictions. The Act established federal standards for insurers, health maintenance organizations (HMOs), and employer plans, including those who self-insure. However, it allowed states and sometimes insurers substantial state flexibility for compliance with the federal requirements.

HIPAA also included tax provisions relating to health insurance. It permitted a limited number of small businesses and self-employed individuals to contribute to tax-advantaged medical savings accounts

---

[+] Excerpted from CRS Report RL31634.

(MSAs) established in conjunction with high-deductible health insurance plans. It increased the deduction for health insurance that self-employed taxpayers may claim. In addition, it allowed long-term care expenses to be treated like deductible medical expenses and clarified the tax treatment of long-term care insurance.

HIPAA amended the Employee Retirement Income Security Act (ERISA), the Public Health Service (PHS) Act, and the Internal Revenue Code (IRC). In general, requirements on employer plans are found in the ERISA and IRC amendments; requirements on health insurance issuers, such as insurance carriers and health maintenance organizations (HMOs) are found in the PHS Act and ERISA amendments. The increased deduction for the self-employed, tax-favored MSAs, and long-term care provisions are amendments to the IRC.

PART I. THE ACT IN GENERAL

The basic intent of HIPAA's health insurance provisions is to lower the possibility that people and small employers will lose existing health plan coverage, and to make it easier for individuals to switch plans or to purchase coverage on their own if they lose employer-offered coverage. The health insurance reforms ensure that people who are moving from one job to another or from employment to unemployment are not denied health insurance because they have a preexisting medical condition (portability) and limit the waiting time before a plan covers any preexisting medical condition for participants and beneficiaries in group health plans.

The reforms also guarantee that individuals and employers who choose to purchase coverage are able to find a plan (guaranteed issue) and that individuals already covered, as well as employers that offer coverage to their employees, are able to renew their coverage (guaranteed renewal). Finally, the health insurance provisions prohibit discrimination on the basis of health status (non-discrimination) and require plans to offer special enrollment periods.

Other HIPAA provisions seek to make health insurance more affordable. The Act raised the tax deduction for health insurance premiums paid by the self-employed. MSAs coupled with qualified high deductible health insurance plans were made available on a trial basis to a limited number of individuals. New tax incentives were made available to encourage individuals and employers to purchase long-term care insurance. Finally, the Act included administrative simplification and privacy provisions instructing the Secretary of HHS to issue standards addressing the electronic transmission of health information and the privacy of personally identifiable medical information.

Additional federal protections have been added since the passage of HIPAA. The protections required plans that cover newborn delivery to allow for a minimum 2-day hospital stay under certain conditions, required plans that offer mental health services to offer them subject to similar limitations as other health benefits, and required plans that cover mastectomy to also cover reconstructive surgery. In addition, the deduction allowed for premium costs for the self-employed was changed.

Does HIPAA Help Individuals who are Uninsured?

HIPAA's insurance provisions were designed to help *insured* Americans who have a preexisting medical condition and have stayed in a job because they fear that they would lose coverage for such a condition if they change to a new employer or move to an individual policy. It also would help those who have been denied the option to purchase insurance as an individual or through their employer because of their health status. They do not address the larger problem of the uninsured, estimated to be 41.2 million people in 2001, although other HIPAA provisions, such as the tax deduction for health insurance costs for self-employed, may encourage some uninsured, self-employed individuals to purchase coverage for themselves.

It is also the case that HIPAA largely addresses the availability of insurance and does not regulate the price of health insurance coverage.[1] Some evidence suggests that the cost of health insurance in the individual market for individuals taking advantage of HIPAA's group-to-individual portability provisions is significantly higher than the cost for individuals who could otherwise obtain insurance. This may be discouraging many "HIPAA eligibles" from buying insurance.[2] Whether this experience continues over the long run remains to be seen.

---

[1] Insurance that is regulated by state law may be subject to state premium limits. There are no premium limits on self-insured employer plans.
[2] U.S. General Accounting Office. Health Insurance Standards. *New Federal Law Creates Challenges for Consumers, Insurers, Regulators.* GAO/HEHS-98-67. February 1998.

Are Employers Required to Offer Health Insurance as a Benefit?

No, the Act does not require employers to offer or pay for health insurance for their employees. Also, the Act does not require employers to offer or pay for family coverage (spouses and dependents). Finally, the Act does not require employers to cover part time, seasonal, or temporary employees. However, an employer who elects to sponsor a group health plan has to comply with certain requirements of the Act. These requirements: (a) restrict the use of preexisting condition limitation periods; (b) prohibit an employer plan from discriminating on the basis of health status in determining the eligibility of an employee to enroll in a group health plan (and the employee's spouse and dependents if the plan provides family coverage); (c) prohibit an employer plan from requiring an individual to pay premiums or contributions which are greater than those charged to a similarly situated individual on the basis of health status; and (d) mandate documentation of creditable coverage.

PART II. HEALTH INSURANCE REFORMS

Portability

HIPAA's "portability" protection means that once a person obtains creditable health plan coverage, he or she can use evidence of that coverage to reduce or eliminate any preexisting medical condition exclusion period that might otherwise be imposed when moving to another health plan. The protections apply when a person moves from one group health plan to another, from a group health plan to an individual policy, or from an individual policy to a group health plan. The concept of portability is really one of being able to maintain coverage and being given *credit* for having been insured when changing health plans. It does *not* mean that an individual can take a specific health insurance policy from one job to another.

What is Creditable Coverage?

The concept of creditable coverage is that individuals are given credit for previous insurance when applying for a new plan.

The Health Insurance Portability and Accountability Act (HIPAA)

Under the Act, creditable coverage is coverage under any of the following: (a) a group health plan; (b) health insurance coverage[3], including individual health insurance coverage; (c) Medicare; (d) Medicaid; (e) military health care;[4] (f) a medical care program of the Indian Health Service or of a tribal organization; (g) a state health benefits risk pool; (h) the Federal Employee Health Benefits Program; (i) a public health plan (as defined in regulations); or (j) a health benefit plan under Section 5(e) of the Peace Corps Act (22 U.S.C. 2504(e)).[5]

What is a Preexisting Medical Condition?

Under the Act, a preexisting medical condition is a physical or mental condition for which medical advice, diagnosis, care, or treatment was recommended or received within the 6-month period ending on the enrollment date. The enrollment date is the date of enrollment of the individual in the plan or, if earlier, the first day of the waiting period for such enrollment.[6] Pregnancy is not considered a preexisting medical condition. Also, a preexisting medical condition limit or exclusion may not be imposed on covered benefits for newborns who are covered under creditable coverage within 30 days of birth. Finally, a preexisting medical condition limit or exclusion may not be imposed on covered benefits for newly adopted children or children newly placed for adoption, if the child becomes covered under creditable coverage within 30 days of the adoption or placement.

The Act also prohibits the use of genetic information as a preexisting condition, unless there is a diagnosis of a preexisting medical condition related to the information. For example, evidence of a positive test for the gene that predisposes a woman to inheritable breast cancer cannot be treated as a preexisting condition, unless a diagnosis of breast cancer is made within the 6-month period described above.

What is a Preexisting Medical Condition Limitation Period?

During this period, a plan may exclude or restrict coverage of a participant's or beneficiary's preexisting medical condition. Under the Act, a

---

[3] Health insurance coverage is defined as benefits consisting of medical care (provided directly, through insurance or reimbursement, or otherwise and including items and services paid for as medical care) under any hospital or medical service policy or certificate, hospital or medical service plan contract or HMD contract offered by a health insurance issuer.

[4] Military health care is care described under Chapter 55 of Title 10 of the United States Code.

[5] Having creditable coverage does not necessarily make an individual eligible for the group to individual market protections. See the question discussing the limitations of those protections on page 8.

[6] See below for more information on limitation and waiting periods.

group health plan is prohibited from imposing more than a 12-month preexisting condition limitation period (18 months for late enrollees) on an HIPAA-eligible participant or beneficiary. As described below, that period is reduced by the amount of the individual's creditable coverage. In the individual market, HIPAA-eligible individuals also have portability protection, although the circumstances under which those protections apply are complex as described in more detail below.

Portability in the Group Market

HIPAA requires *group health plans* (plans that are offered to an employment-based group - including both employers and employee organizations) that are covered by the Act to meet the following requirements related to portability:

- When a person with prior creditable coverage first enrolls in a group health plan, the plan cannot impose a limitation period on a preexisting condition that is longer than 12 months (18 months for late enrollees as defined below). The length of the allowed preexisting condition limitation period is based on any *creditable coverage* that an individual may have. The plan cannot apply any preexisting condition waiting period on pregnancy, a covered newborn, or on any covered child under 18 who is adopted (even if the adoption is not finalized). However, the employer may still require individuals to work for a period of time before they are allowed to participate in the health plan. This is called a "waiting period" and should not be confused with a "preexisting condition limitation period."[7]

- Employers who sponsor group health plans are required to provide enrollees with a certificate that states the amount of creditable coverage accumulated and whether or not the enrollee was subject to a waiting period under the employer's plan. Individuals can use this certificate to demonstrate prior creditable coverage when moving to a new group or individual health insurance plan. The Act does not require an employer to continue offering coverage to

---

[7] See below for more information on limitation and waiting periods.

enrollees who have left their jobs, except under COBRA continuation provisions as described below.

How do People Take Full Advantage of the Portability Provisions of the Act?

To benefit from the Act, individuals should maintain coverage under a health insurance plan without experiencing significant lapses in coverage. Since the portability protection only applies to people with "continuous coverage", which the statute defines as coverage with no lapses of 63 or more days, individuals should not allow their insurance coverage to lapse for 63 or more days.

How Long can a Group Health Plan Restrict Coverage for a Preexisting Medical Condition?

Coverage of a preexisting medical condition may be limited or excluded for up to 12 months for those who enroll in a health plan when first eligible to enroll. In the case of late enrollment, the maximum permitted limitation is 18 months.

For those moving from one group plan to another group plan, or from individual to group coverage, the new plan must reduce any preexisting condition limitation period by 1 month for every month that such individuals had creditable coverage under a previous plan, provided that they enroll when first eligible and had no break in previous coverage of 63 or more continuous days. For example, individuals with 6 months of prior creditable coverage could face a maximum preexisting condition limitation period of 6 months. Individuals with 11 months of prior creditable coverage could face a maximum limitation period of 1 month. Once a 12-month limitation period is met, no new limitation may ever be imposed *as long as continuous coverage is maintained* (that is, there is no break in coverage lasting longer than 62 days), even if there is a change in jobs or health plans. If there is a period of 63 consecutive days during which individuals have no creditable coverage, they may be subject to as much as a 12-month preexisting condition exclusion period (or an 18 month exclusion for late enrollees).[8]

Individuals establish eligibility for a waiver of preexisting condition limitations by presenting certifications that document prior creditable coverage. Health plans and health insurance issuers must supply written certifications of: the period of creditable coverage under the plan; coverage (if any) under COBRA continuation provisions; and any waiting or

---

[8] See "What is Late Enrollment?" below.

affiliation periods imposed. The certification must be provided: (1) when a participant is no longer covered under the plan or otherwise becomes covered under a COBRA continuation provision; (2) after termination of COBRA coverage, if applicable; and (3) upon a request which is made not later then 24 months after coverage ends. The interim rules issued by the three agencies administering the Act provide guidance and model certification forms to streamline this process.[9] In general, the certification must be provided in writing.

What is Late Enrollment?

Late enrollment occurs when an individual enrolls in a group health plan other than during: (a) the first period in which the individual is eligible to enroll under the plan, or (b) a special enrollment period. As described above, a group health plan may require a late enrollee to wait 18 months before a preexisting condition is covered.

What is a Waiting Period? How does it Differ from a Preexisting Condition Limitation Period?

A waiting period is a set amount of time an employee must wait before he or she is eligible to enroll in a health plan. For example, an employer may require an employee to work for 6 months before health insurance benefits become available. The Act does not limit this type of waiting period - employers and health insurance issuers are free to determine the length of a waiting period. However, the Act requires that any waiting period be applied uniformly without regard to the health status of potential plan participants or beneficiaries. Also, days in a waiting period are not taken into account when determining whether an individual has experienced a break in coverage of 63 or more days.

This differs from a preexisting condition exclusion limitation period which allows plans to exclude coverage for certain preexisting health conditions for up to 12 months (or 18 months), as described above. *Any waiting period required before an employee or his or family member can become a plan participant or beneficiary must run concurrently with any preexisting condition limitation period.* For example, if an employer required an employee without any creditable coverage to work for 5 months before he or she could enroll in the firm's health plan, then the preexisting condition limitation period imposed on the coverage of that individual could not exceed 7 months from the date of actual enrollment in the plan. If that

---

[9] *Federal Register*, April 8, 1997.

individual had 7 or more months of creditable coverage, then no preexisting condition limitation period could be imposed on the coverage under the new plan.

Do Plans and Issuers have any Discretion in the Method of Crediting Prior Coverage?

Yes, when an individual changes plans, the new benefit package may cover some benefits that were not covered under his or her most recent prior plan, and the law allows the new plan or issuer some discretion in applying prior creditable coverage to those new benefits. Plans and issuers may choose between two alternatives when determining creditable coverage: 1) they can chose to include all periods of coverage from qualified sources and thus not look at any specific benefits; or 2) they can examine prior coverage on a benefit-specific basis, and are allowed to exclude from creditable coverage any categories or classes of benefits not covered under the most recent prior plan. The April 8, 1997 interim rule defines the categories of benefits that may be considered separately to be: (a) mental health; (b) substance abuse treatment; (c) prescription drugs; (d) dental care; or (e) vision care.[10] Thus, for example, if a prior plan did not cover prescription drugs, and the new plan includes this benefit, the new plan may exclude coverage of prescription drugs for up to 12 months under this second method. If the second method is chosen, plans or issuers must disclose its use at the time of enrollment or sale of the plan, and apply it uniformly.

Do these Protections Apply to an Individual's Spouse and Children?

Under a group health plan, an employer is not required to offer coverage to an individual's spouse or children. If the employer does offer family coverage, the same protections apply to a spouse and dependents. Coverage may not be denied because a family member is sick, and preexisting condition restrictions are limited as described above.

Portability and Guaranteed Availability in the Individual Insurance Market

HIPAA guarantees the availability of a plan and prohibits pre-existing condition exclusions for certain eligible individuals who are moving from group health insurance to insurance in the individual market. States have the

---

[10] *Ibid.,* p. 16932, 16945-6, 16961-2.

choice of either enforcing the HIPAA individual market guarantees, referred to as the "federal fallback", or they may establish an "acceptable alternative state mechanism". In states using the federal fallback approach, HIPAA requires all health insurance issuers operating in the individual health insurance market to offer coverage to *all eligible individuals* and prohibits them from placing any limitations on the coverage of any preexisting medical condition.

Issuers can comply with the Act's requirements in three ways:

(1) they must offer eligible individuals access to coverage to every individual insurance policy they sell in the state; or

(2) they must offer eligible individuals access to coverage to their two most popular insurance policies (based on premium volume); or

(3) they must offer eligible individuals access to a lower-level and higher-level coverage. These two policies must include benefits that are substantially similar to other coverage offered by the issuer in the state, and must include risk adjustment, risk spreading, or financial subsidization.

Issuers can refuse to cover individuals seeking portability from the group market if financial or provider capacity would be impaired. This means, for example, that if a network-based plan like an HMO can demonstrate that it is filled to capacity, then it would not have to accept eligible individuals. It would have to apply this exception uniformly, without regard to the health status of applicants.

Who is Eligible for Group to Individual Market Portability and Guaranteed Availability under the Act?

An eligible individual must have:

- creditable health insurance coverage for 18 months or longer;
- most recent coverage under a traditional employer group plan, governmental plan, or church plan;
- exhausted any COBRA (or other continuation) coverage;[11]
- no eligibility for coverage under any employment-based plan, Medicare or Medicaid; and

---

[11] Individuals may have continuation coverage that is not COBRA coverage under FEHBP or under state continuation of coverage laws.

- no breaks in coverage of 63 or more days.[12]

Individuals purchasing insurance on their own who do not meet these eligibility criteria, are not protected by HIPAA's portability and guaranteed availability provisions. These individuals may be protected under state laws.

What are the Limitations of the Group-to-Individual Portability and guaranteed Availability Protections?

The group-to-individual portability and guaranteed availability protections apply only to individuals whose most recent coverage was provided through traditional employer-based group arrangements, governmental plans or church-sponsored plans. Group plans are defined as those meeting the ERISA definition, which is limited to those sponsored through a traditional employer-employee relationship or an employment-based association. Governmental plans are also defined in ERISA. They are plans that are established or maintained for its employees by the Government of the United States, the government of a state or a political subdivision of a state. This limitation means that people whose most recent coverage was sponsored by the military (CHAMPUS and TRICARE), many college-sponsored student plans, the Peace Corps, the Veterans' Administration, the Indian Health Service, Medicare, Medicaid and SCHIP are not eligible for the federal group-to-individual portability and guaranteed availability protections. (Although states may offer these individuals such protections.)

What are the Requirements for an Acceptable Alternative State Mechanism?

An acceptable alternative state mechanism for coverage of eligible individuals must:

- provide a choice of health insurance coverage to all eligible individuals;
- not impose any preexisting condition restrictions; and
- include at least one policy form of coverage that is comparable to either comprehensive health insurance coverage offered in the

---

[12] An eligible individual must have 18 months of creditable health insurance coverage, at least the last day of which was under a group health plan. A child is deemed to be an eligible individual if the child was covered under any creditable coverage within 30 days of birth, adoption, or placement for adoption, and the child has not had a break in coverage of 63 or more days. (Issuers are not required, however, to offer family coverage.) *Federal Register*, April 8, 1997. p. 16996.

individual market in the state, or a standard option of coverage available under the group or individual health insurance laws in the state.

In addition to these requirements, a state may implement one of the following mechanisms:

- certain National Association of Insurance Commissioners (NAIC) Model Acts;[13]
- a qualified high risk pool[14] that meets certain specified requirements; or
- other risk spreading or risk adjustment approach, or financial subsidies for participating insurers or eligible individuals; or
- any other mechanism under which eligible individuals are provided a choice of all individual health insurance coverage otherwise available.

Examples of potential alternative state mechanisms include health insurance coverage pools or programs, mandatory group conversion policies, guaranteed issue of one or more plans of individual health insurance coverage, open enrollment by one or more health insurance issuers, or a combination of such mechanisms.

How have States Implemented this Provision?

Table 1 provides information on how each state has implemented the Act's group-to-individual portability provisions. As of December 2001, the District of Columbia and 10 states (Arizona, Delaware, Hawaii, Maryland, Missouri, Nevada, North Carolina, Rhode Island, Tennessee, and West Virginia) utilize the federal fallback mechanism. Missouri is also the only state that does not enforce these standards itself, and as a result CMS is responsible for enforcement in Missouri. As shown in Table 1, many states have elected to provide group-to-individual portability through high-risk pools, while others utilize a combination of high-risk pools, existing state

---

[13] The NAIC Model Acts include the Small Employer and Individual Health Insurance Availability Model Act, as it applies to individual health insurance coverage, and as revised in state regulations to meet all the necessary requirements and the Individual Health Insurance Portability Model Act, as adopted on June 3, 1996 and revised in state regulation to meet all necessary requirements.

[14] A high risk pool is generally the insurer of last resort, typically for sicker and/or older individuals who: 1) are denied coverage in the private market; 2) are offered only restricted coverage; or 3) cannot find less expensive coverage.

insurance reform laws, or other mechanisms. To obtain more information on a state's health insurance regulation of the individual market, individuals may wish to contact that state's department of insurance.

Table 1. State Group-to-Individual Insurance Portability Mechanisms

State	Group-to-Individual Insurance Portability Provision
Alabama	Alternative mechanism - high-risk health insurance pool.
Alaska	Alternative mechanism - high-risk health insurance pool.
Arizona	Federal fall-back.
Arkansas	Alternative mechanism - high-risk health insurance pool.
California	Alternate mechanism - plans must offer two most popular products.
Colorado	Alternative mechanism - high-risk health insurance pool.
Connecticut	Alternative mechanism - high-risk health insurance pool.
Delaware	Federal fall-back.
District of Columbia	Federal fall-back.
Florida	Alternative mechanism - guaranteed issue to HIPAA-eligible persons. Health plans required to offer a choice of conversion plans, one of which must be the state approved "standard policy" currently offered in the small group market.
Georgia	Alternative mechanism - assigned risk pool. HIPAA-eligible persons may apply for coverage to the Insurance Commissioner who then "assigns" eligible individuals to health plans based on a health plan's pro rata volume of individual health insurance business done in the state.
Hawaii	Federal fall-back.
Idaho	Alternative mechanism - existing state insurance reform laws, including: guaranteed issue of three products (basic, standard, and catastrophic), guaranteed renewal, preexisting condition limitations of 12/6, and also retains pregnancy as a preexisting condition *(not in compliance with HIPAA)*, coverage gap is 63 days, rating bands to limit rate variations to a range of 1.7 to 1 for experience, health status and duration and allows demographic adjustments for age and gender.
Illinois	Alternative mechanism - high-risk health insurance pool.
Indiana	Alternative mechanism - high-risk health insurance pool.
Iowa	Alternative mechanism - high-risk health insurance pool.
Kansas	Alternative mechanism - high-risk health insurance pool.
Kentucky	Alternative mechanism - high-risk health insurance pool.
Louisiana	Alternative mechanism - high-risk health insurance pool.
Maine	Alternative mechanism - existing state insurance reform laws, including: guaranteed issue of all products, guaranteed renewal, no preexisting condition waiting period applied to HIPAA-eligibles and 12/6 for non-HIPAA eligibles, coverage gap of 63 days, community rating with adjustments limited to a range of 1.5 to 1 for age, smoking status, industry, and geography.
Maryland	Federal fall-back.

State	Group-to-Individual Insurance Portability Provision
Massachusetts	Alternate mechanism- existing state insurance reform laws, including: guaranteed issue of three products, guaranteed renewal, preexisting condition limitations of 6/6 and coverage gap of 63 days, modified community rating with adjustments for age, geography and benefit level limited to a range of 2 to 1.
Michigan	Alternate mechanism- Blue Cross Blue Shield plan will enroll HIPAA eligibles.
Minnesota	Alternative mechanism - high-risk health insurance pool.
Mississippi	Alternative mechanism- high-risk health insurance pool.
Missouri	Federal fall-back with CMS enforcement.
Montana	Alternative mechanism - high-risk health insurance pool.
Nebraska	Alternative mechanism - high-risk health insurance pool.
Nevada	Federal fall-back.
New Hampshire	Alternative mechanism - high-risk health insurance pool.
New Jersey	Alternative mechanism - existing state insurance law, including: guaranteed issue of five standardized products, guaranteed renewal, no preexisting condition waiting period applied to HIPAA eligibles (for all others preexisting condition limitations of 12/6), coverage gap of 30 days, pure community rating.
New Mexico	Alternative mechanism - HIPAA-eligibles can choose to obtain coverage through either the high-risk health insurance pool or the purchasing alliance.
New York	Alternative mechanism - existing state insurance reform laws, including: guaranteed issue of all products, guaranteed renewal, no preexisting condition waiting period applied to HIPAA eligibles (for all others preexisting condition limitations of 12/6), coverage gap of 63 days, community rating with adjustments permitted for family composition and geographic regions.
North Carolina	Federal fall-back.
North Dakota	Alternative mechanism- high-risk health insurance pool.
Ohio	Alternative mechanism- separate open enrollment period for HIPAA eligibles until health plans meet their enrollment caps.
Oklahoma	Alternative mechanism - high-risk health insurance pool.
Oregon	Alternative mechanism - high-risk health insurance pool.
Pennsylvania	Alternative mechanism - Blue Cross and Blue Shield Plans serve as the guaranteed issue carrier.
Rhode Island	Federal fall-back.
South Carolina	Alternative mechanism- high-risk health insurance pool.
South Dakota	Alternative mechanism - existing state insurance reform laws, including: guaranteed issue to HIPAA-eligibles until these enrollees represent 2% of annual earned premium, guaranteed renewal, preexisting condition limitations to 12/6, and also retains pregnancy as a preexisting condition

State	Group-to-Individual Insurance Portability Provision
	(not in compliance with HIPAA), coverage gap is 63 days, rating reform limits adjustments for health status and claims experience to 2.2 to 1.
Tennessee	Federal fall-back.
Texas	Alternative mechanism - high-risk health insurance pool.
Utah	Alternative mechanism- combines high-risk health insurance pool and existing insurance market guaranteed issue requirement. Individuals who are denied coverage by a plan and then are judged by objective guidelines to be "too healthy" must be covered by the health plan that had previously denied their coverage. Individuals who are not deemed "too healthy" would be eligible for coverage in the high-risk pool.
Vermont	Alternative mechanism - existing state insurance reform laws, including: guaranteed issue of all products, guaranteed renewal, no preexisting condition waiting period applied to HIPAA eligibles (for all others preexisting condition limitations of 12/12), coverage gap of 63 days, community rating with health plans required to limit rating adjustments to a range of 1.5 to 1 for one or more factors approved by the Commissioner.
Virginia	Alternative mechanism- guaranteed issue of all currently offered non-group products to HIPAA eligibles.
Washington	Alternative mechanism - high-risk health insurance pool.
West Virginia	Federal fall-back.
Wisconsin	Alternative mechanism- high-risk health insurance pool.
Wyoming	Alternative mechanism- high-risk health insurance pool.

Source: Blue Cross and Blue Shield Association, *State Legislative Health Care and Insurance Issues. 2001 Survey of Plans.* Washington, December 2001.

Note: (1) For preexisting condition limitations there may be two numbers, such as 12/6. The first number denotes the exclusion period and the second number denotes the allowable look-back period. The federal maximum under HIPAA is 12/6, although states may impose shorter limits. (2) Additionally, for coverage gaps, HIPAA requires that all periods of creditable coverage be aggregated or combined, provided that the lapse between periods of coverage is less than 63 days. Individual states may require health plans to give credit for prior coverage even if the lapse was longer than 63 days. (3) Rating bands are laws that restrict a plan's use of experience, health status or duration of coverage in setting premiums rates for individuals. For example, a state may set the band of 2 to 1 for health status.

Special Enrollment Periods in the Group Market

As an adjunct to its portability requirement, the Act provides for two different special enrollment periods to ensure that people losing group health insurance coverage can more easily obtain other group coverage when it is available. The two special enrollment periods are:

(1) Individual Losing Other Coverage

A group health plan or an issuer offering coverage in connection with a group health plan must allow an employee who is eligible, but not enrolled, to become covered under the plan if the following conditions are met:[15]

- The employee or dependent was covered under a group health plan or had health insurance coverage at the time coverage was previously offered to the employee or dependent. For example, the employee may have been covered by a spouse's employer and declined coverage under his own employer's plan.

- The employee stated in writing at the time of declining enrollment that the reason for declining was that he or she was covered under another health insurance plan. This condition applies only if the plan sponsor or issuer requires such a written statement.

- The employee's or dependent's previous coverage was under a COBRA continuation provision that had become exhausted or was under some other coverage that had been terminated as a result of a loss of eligibility for the coverage (for reasons such as: legal separation, divorce, death, termination of employment, or reduction in the number of hours of employment), or because the employer contribution towards such coverage was terminated.

To take advantage of a special enrollment period, the employee would have to request enrollment no later than 30 days after the date in which his or her prior coverage was exhausted or terminated.

(2) Dependent Beneficiaries

This special enrollment period applies to individuals who become dependents through marriage, birth, adoption, or placement of adoption. Generally, this provision applies if a group health plan makes dependent coverage available, and the new dependent's spouse or parent is either a participant or *eligible* (including meeting any waiting periods) to be a participant under the plan. The newly dependent individual must be allowed to enroll as a beneficiary under the plan; however, enrollment must be sought within 30 days of the qualifying event (e.g., the marriage). Employees or spouses who are eligible, but not previously enrolled in the

---

[15] The employee's dependent would also be allowed to enroll, if family coverage is provided under the terms of the plan.

plan, may also enroll during this special enrollment. Coverage is effective on the date of the birth, adoption, or placement for adoption. In the case of marriage, coverage is effective no later than the first day of the month beginning after the date the request for enrollment is received.

Non-Discrimination in the Group Market

Can a Group Health Plan Refuse to Enroll Individuals with a History of Illness or Disability or High Medical Expenses? Can it Drop Someone from Coverage who becomes Sick or Starts Using a lot of Medical Care?

No, the Act prohibits a group health plan and an issuer offering group health coverage from establishing rules for eligibility for any individual to enroll under the plan based on health status-related factors.[16] These factors include: health status, medical condition (including both physical and mental illnesses), claims experience, receipt of health care, medical history, genetic information, evidence of insurability (including conditions arising out of domestic violence) and disability. Group health plans are also prohibited from failing to re-enroll a participant or beneficiary on the basis of health status-related factors. HIPAA also prohibits plans from charging differential premiums for enrollees within a group plan based on these health status-related factors.

Can an Employer Condition Coverage under its Health Plan on Passing a Physical Examination?

No, the Act prohibits employer plans and issuers of group health coverage from establishing rules of eligibility to enroll under the terms of the plan that discriminate based on one or more health-status related factors.

Can a Group Plan Refuse to Enroll Individuals who Engage in High Risk Recreational Activities?

No, these individuals cannot be denied enrollment in a group health plan, based on HIPAA's non-discrimination provision. Group plans or issuers offering group health coverage cannot use information about an individual's health status to either deny coverage or charge differential

---

[16] In the individual market there are no federal rules explicitly limiting denials based on health status. On the other hand, portability and guaranteed issue protections may apply (see above section on Portability and Guaranteed Availability in the Individual Insurance Market).

premiums. On January 8, 2001, the Department of Labor issued a preliminary final ruling with comment period, defining the nondiscrimination provisions of HIPAA. In this ruling, health status is defined very broadly to include "evidence of insurability" which in turn includes a provision that prohibits excluding coverage for individuals who participate in high-risk activities.[17] Thus, this broad interpretation extends the nondiscrimination protections to individuals who engage high risk recreational activities.

Can a Group Plan Exclude Coverage of Treatments for Injuries Obtained while Engaging in High Risk Recreational Activities?

HIPAA'S protection extend to enrollment policies and premiums. The protection does not address the benefits that are covered by these plans. Therefore, there is no federal requirement to cover treatments for injuries associated with high risk activities, even if these treatments are otherwise covered under the plan. For example, a plan may exclude coverage for a broken leg, if it occurs as a result of a high risk activity.

Do these Non-Discrimination Protections Apply to an Individual's Spouse and Children?

Under a group health plan, an employer is not required to offer coverage to an individual's spouse or children. If the employer does offer family coverage, the same non-discrimination protections apply to a spouse and dependents. Coverage may not be denied because a family member is sick, and preexisting condition restrictions are limited as described above.

Does the Act Restrict the Premium Amounts that an Employer can Charge for Health Insurance?

No, the Act does not restrict premium amounts that an employer or insurer can charge. It also expressly permits an employer or group health insurer to offer premium discounts or rebates, or modify otherwise applicable copayments or deductibles, for participation in health promotion and disease prevention programs. However, the Act does prohibit a health plan from charging an individual a higher premium than the premium

---

[17] This ruling stems from language in the conference report on HIPAA. "The inclusion of evidence of insurability in the definition of health status is intended to ensure, among other things, that individuals are not excluded from health care coverage due to their participation in activities such as motorcycling, snowmobiling, all-terrain vehicle riding, horseback riding, skiing, and other similar activities." (Conference Report, H. Rept 104-736, 104th Cong., 2d Sess. 186 (1996)).

charged for another similarly situated individual enrolled in the plan on the basis of any health-related factor, such as a preexisting medical condition.

Guaranteed Issue and Guaranteed Renewability

The Act requires insurers, HMOs, and other issuers of health insurance selling in the *small group market* to accept any small employer that applies for coverage, regardless of the health status or claims history of the employer's group.[18] This requirement is often referred to as "guaranteed issue." The Act defines a small employer as one with two to 50 employees. (If, on the first day of the plan year, the plan has fewer than two participants who are current employees, it is not considered a small group and would not be covered by this "guaranteed issue" requirement.) Under guaranteed issue, the issuer must accept for enrollment under the policy, not just the employer's group, as a whole, but also every eligible individual in the employers' group who is eligible for and applies for timely enrollment.[19] Exceptions to guaranteed issue are provided in the Act for network plans that might otherwise exceed capacity limits or in the event that the employer's employees do not live, work, or reside in the network plan's area.

Employer groups with more than 50 employees are not protected by this requirement unless otherwise required under state law. In the past, health insurance issuers usually did not examine the health status or medical history of larger employer groups when deciding whether to accept such groups for coverage. The Act requires the Secretary of Health and Human Services (HHS) and the General Accounting Office to report every 3 years, beginning in December 2002, on access to health insurance in the large group market.

Can Health Insurance Issuers Drop or Cancel Coverage for Groups because of High Medical Costs?

No, the Act requires all health insurance issuers to continue coverage for any group, regardless of health status or use of services, if the group requests renewal. This requirement is known as guaranteed renewability. An issuer may drop coverage in cases of non-payment of premiums, fraud, or similar

---

[18] This is consistent with most state health insurance reforms which primarily apply to the small group market (typically defined as 2 to 25, 2 to 35 or 2 to 50 employees). However, some state laws provide for guaranteed issue of groups with as few as one employee.
[19] The interim rules interpret the guaranteed issue requirement to apply to all products actively marketed by an issuer in the small group market. *Federal Register,* April 8, 1997. p. 16971.

reasons not related to health status, such as violation of participation or contribution rules.[20] But, there are no limits on amounts insurers may charge.

Federally Required Benefits

As originally passed, HIPAA did not require an employer or issuer of group health insurance to offer specific benefits. Twice since its passage Congress added to HIPAA's protections by mandating specific benefits, but in each case only for plans that cover certain services. Legislation enacted in 1997, as a part of an unrelated appropriations bill,[21] included provisions that: (1) require plans that cover mental health services to provide limited mental health "parity", and (2) prohibit plans that cover newborn delivery from limiting hospital stays for newborn delivery to less than 2 days. Legislation enacted in 1998 requires plans that cover mastectomy as a treatment for breast cancer to also cover reconstructive surgery.[22]

Mental Health Parity

Private health insurers often provide less coverage for the treatment of mental illnesses than they do for the treatment of other illnesses. For example, health plans may limit treatment of mental illnesses by covering fewer hospital days and outpatient office visits, and increase cost sharing for mental health care by raising deductibles and copayments. Twenty-three states have passed full-parity laws that require health plans to impose the same treatment limitations and financial requirements on their mental health coverage as they do on their medical and surgical coverage. Other states have enacted legislation that requires health plans to provide certain specified mental health benefits (but not full parity). However, these laws do not apply to self-insured employers, which are exempt from state regulation under ERISA.

In 1996, Congress passed the Mental Health Parity Act (MHPA), which amended ERISA and the Public Health Service Act to establish new federal

---

[20] An example of a participation rule is a requirement set by the issuer that 80% of all full time employees participate in the employer's group health plan. An example of a contribution requirement is that all participants in the health plan must pay 20% of the plan premium. These requirements are used to protect the issuer from a selection bias (also known as "adverse selection") in which only sick members of an employer's group sign up for insurance coverage.

[21] FY1997 appropriations bill for the Departments of Veterans' Affairs and Housing and Urban Development (P.L. 104-204, Title VII).

[22] In addition to HIPAA's limited federal protections, most states have their own mandates for insurers operating in their states.

standards for mental health coverage offered by employer-sponsored plans.[23] Identical provisions were later added to the Internal Revenue Code.[24] The MHPA is limited in scope and does not compel insurers to provide full-parity coverage. For group plans that choose to offer mental health benefits, the MHPA requires parity only for annual and lifetime dollar limits on coverage. Plans may still impose more restrictive treatment limitations and cost sharing requirements on their mental health coverage. The MHPA includes several other limitations. Employers with 50 or fewer employees are exempt from the law. In addition, employers that experience an increase in claims costs of at least 1% as a result of MHPA compliance can apply for an exemption.

In 2001, Congress tried unsuccessfully to enact legislation (S. 543) that would amend and expand the MHPA by requiring plans that choose to offer mental health benefits to provide full-parity coverage. Lawmakers instead reauthorized the MHPA through December 31, 2002. On April 29, 2002, President Bush urged Congress to enact S. 543, which enjoys broad support among lawmakers and patient advocacy groups. Employers and health insurance organizations oppose S. 543 because of concerns that it will drive up health care costs.

Newborns' and Mothers' Health Protection Act

The Newborns' and Mothers' Health Protection Act was also passed as part of P.L. 104-204. This Act prohibits group health plans and issuers offering group coverage from restricting the hospital length of stay for childbirth for either the mother or newborn child to less than 48 hours for normal deliveries and to less than 96 hours for caesarian deliveries.

Women's Health and Cancer Rights Act of 1998

Enacted in 1998, Title IX of H.R. 4328, the Omnibus Appropriations bill for fiscal year 1999[25] required group plans and health insurance issuers providing coverage in connection with a group plan that provide medical and surgical benefits related to mastectomy to cover breast reconstruction procedures, as well. The provision included a requirement that beneficiaries be notified of available coverage for prostheses and treatment of physical complications of reconstructive procedures.

---

[23] P.L. 104-204, Title VII, codified at 29 U.S.C. 1185a and 42 U.S.C. 300gg-5. These provisions were part of the FY1997 VA-HUD appropriations bill.
[24] P.L. 105-34, Section 1531(a)(4), codified at 26 U.S.C. 9812.
[25] P.L. 105-277, Title DC: Women's Health and Cancer Rights.

Can an Employer Exclude Coverage for Specific Types of Illnesses, such as Cancer, or Acquired Immune Deficiency Syndrome (AIDS) or Treatment of Injuries Associated with High Risk Activities?

Federal law does not prohibit employers from excluding treatment of specific illnesses or conditions from their health benefit plans. On the other hand, a number of factors limit certain employers' ability to exclude specific illnesses from coverage. Most states have enacted legislation requiring that specific benefits or coverage be included in insured products. In addition, employers purchasing insurance products often have little or no discretion in choosing or excluding specific types of services or procedures. This is because many insurance companies and HMOs have a set menu of products that do not vary considerably from one employer group to another. For self-funded plans, however, ERISA prevents state laws from applying and benefits are crafted by each individual employer plan. Thus only the few federal requirements enacted in HIPAA and its amendments (described above) place specific coverage requirements on these self-funded plans.

General Questions about the Health Insurance Reforms

Do the Requirements of the Act apply to the Plans of Employers that Provide for Dental-Only Coverage or Vision-Only Coverage?

No, such specific benefit plans do not have to comply with the requirements of the Act if they meet certain conditions spelled out in the Act. To be exempt, for example, the dental-only policy would have to be provided under a separate policy, certificate, or contract of insurance or not otherwise be an integral part of the plan.

Do the Requirements of the Act apply to Association-Sponsored Group Health Plans?

Yes, association plans must comply with the various requirements of the Act relating to group health coverage. For example, the sponsor of an association plan cannot drop a group from coverage because of the use of medical services by the group's members. Moreover, the association plan must comply with the restrictions on the use of preexisting medical condition limitation periods, provide for creditable coverage, and renew coverage except in limited cases. However, nothing under the Act requires that an association plan accept for coverage individuals who are *not* members of the association.

Can States Impose Requirements on Insurers Selling to Group Health Plans that are Different from those in the Act?

Yes, states may impose their own requirements. But HIPAA ensures that state laws do not prevent the application of its consumer protections. For example, state laws regulating rating continue to apply because the Act generally does not address rating practices. On the other hand, the Act's provisions relating to portability, such as restrictions on the use of preexisting medical condition limitation periods override state laws. Exceptions include specific types of state laws that provide *for greater portability,* such as state laws that:

- define a preexisting medical condition to be one that existed for less than 6 months prior to becoming covered (instead of the 6 months required under the Act);

- provide for preexisting medical condition limitation periods shorter than 12 (and 18) months in the Act; and

- allow for breaks in continuous coverage longer than the 62-day period specified under the Act.[26]

Thus, for example, a state may prohibit issuers selling to group health plans from imposing more than a 6-month preexisting medical condition limitation period on enrollees, instead of the 12-month limit in the Act. However, state laws that allowed such limitation periods in excess of 12 months would be overridden by the requirement of the Act.

Do the Insurance Reforms apply to Federal Employee's Health Benefits Plans (FEHBP)?

While there are no specific references in HIPAA or the subsequent benefits mandates that apply the requirements specifically to FEHBP, the plans provided by the FEHBP program are presumed to fall under the HIPAA definition of "group health plan." As a result, the federal Office of Personnel Management, which administers the FEHBP program, complies with the HIPAA requirements.

---

[26] Other possible types of state laws providing for greater consumer protections are also specified in the Act

Does the Act Regulate the Premium Amount that an Issuer can Charge an Eligible Individual?

No, the Act does not place any restrictions on the premium amount that issuers can charge. However, some states limit insurance premiums in the individual market and more may decide to do so in the future. Such limits would then apply because the Act does not preempt or override either current or future state laws regulating the cost of insurance.

Implementation and Enforcement

The Secretaries of HHS, Labor, and Treasury are required to jointly enforce the provisions of the Act. The Secretary of Labor enforces the requirements on employer plans under Title I of ERISA. The Secretary of Labor is also generally given authority to promulgate regulations necessary to carry out the provisions of the Act relating to group health plans and health insurance issuers in connection with any group health plan. The Secretary of Treasury enforces requirements on all group health plans under the Internal Revenue Code. Requirements on health insurance issuers (such as insurance carriers and HMOs) are enforced by the Secretary of HHS to the extent that such requirements are not enforced by the states. The Secretaries are required to coordinate their activities to avoid duplication of effort.

States have the primary responsibility for enforcing HIPAA's access, portability and renewability standards applying to insurers in both the group and individual markets. If they do not pass laws that substantially enforce these standards, however, DHHS must do the enforcing itself As of 2001, only Missouri had not enacted enabling legislation.

How are the Insurance Requirements of the Act Enforced?

Noncomplying group health plans covered under ERISA may be subject to civil money penalties, and both plans and issuers can be sued by participants and beneficiaries to recover any benefits due under the plan. The Secretary of Labor has the investigative authority to determine compliance with the law's requirements. For group health plans, generally the IRS can fine a noncomplying employer $100 per day per violation.

Requirements on issuers will be enforced by the states. For Missouri, the Secretary of HHS enforces the provisions. The Secretary may impose a fine of $100 for each day the entity (the issuer or a nonfederal governmental plan)[27] is out of compliance. The Act gives the Secretary of HHS the authority to promulgate regulations needed to carry out the provisions of the Act relating to requirements on issuers of coverage.

What Regulations have been Promulgated to define HIPAA?

The following table lists the regulations regarding HIPAA's insurance provisions.

COBRA Continuation Coverage

How does COBRA Continuation Coverage[28] Interact with HIPAA?

A person's COBRA continuation coverage is considered *creditable coverage* in the case of an individual who moves from one group policy to another group policy or from a group policy to an individual policy. This allows an individual to move from COBRA to a new health plan without having to wait for coverage of any preexisting medical condition under the new plan, providing the individual does not have a lapse in coverage of 63 or more days.

With respect to HIPAA's individual market protections, the situation is somewhat more complex. One of the requirements for eligibility for guaranteed availability and portability in the individual market is that an individual must first have elected and exhausted any available COBRA or other continuation coverage. Eligible individuals who do not have access to COBRA or other continuation coverage may move directly to the individual market. Additionally, in the individual market, it is important to note that the insurer accepting the eligible individual for coverage can charge whatever rate is allowed under state law. (The Act does not limit the premiums that insurers can charge.)

---

[27] "A nonfederal governmental plan" is a plan sponsored by a state or local governmental entity.
[28] The Consolidated Omnibus Budget Reconciliation Act of 1985 (COBRA, P.L. 99-272) requires employers with 20 or more employees to offer continued group health insurance coverage to employees and their dependents after certain events. See CRS Report RL30626, *Health Insurance Continuation Coverage under COBRA*, by Heidi G. Yacker.

Table 2. HIPAA'S Insurance Regulations

Date of Issue	Title	Purpose	Status	Citation
April 8, 1997	Health Insurance Portability for Group Health Plans; Interim Rules and Proposed Rule	Interim rules governing access, portability and renewability requirements for group health plans and issuers of health insurance coverage offered in connection with a group health plan.	Comment period ended July 7, 1997	Internal Revenue Service (IRS): 26 CFR Part 54 Pension Welfare Benefits Administration (PWBA): 29 CFR Part 2590 Health Care Financing Administration (HCFA): 45 CFR Subtitle A, Parts 144 and 146, 45 CFR Part 148
April 8, 1997	Individual Market Health Insurance Reform; Interim final rale with comment period	Portability from group to individual coverage; federal rules for access in the individual market; state alternative mechanisms to federal rules	Comment period ended July 7, 1997	Health Care Financing Administration (HCFA): 45 CFR Part 148
December 22, 1997	Mental Health Parity; Interim Rules HIPAA Mental Health Parity Act; Proposed Rule	Interim rules governing parity between medical/surgical benefits and mental health benefits in group health plans and health insurance coverage offered by issuers in connection with a group health plan.	Comment period ended on March 23, 1998	IRS: 26 CFR Part 54 PWBA: 29 CFR Part 2590 HCFA: 45 CFR Part 146
December 29, 1997	Application of HIPAA Group Market Portability Rules to Health Flexible Spending Arrangements; Final Rule Application of HIPAA Group Market Rules to Individuals Who Were Denied Coverage Due to a Health Status-Related Factor; Final Rule	Clarification of regulations with respect to treatment of benefits under flexible spending arrangements for the purposes of group market portability.	Final (clarifies regulation issued April 8, 1997)	IRS: 26 CFR Part 54 PWBA: 29 CFR Part 2590 HCFA: 45 CFR Parts 144 and 146

Date of Issue	Title	Purpose	Status	Citation
October 27, 1998	Group Health Plans and Health Insurance Issuers Under the Newborns' and Mothers' Health Protection Act; Joint Interim Rule	Interim rules providing guidance to employers, group health plans, health insurance issuers, and participants and beneficiaries relating to new requirements for hospital lengths of stay in connection with childbirth.	Comment period ended January 25, 1999	IRS: 26 CFR Part 54 PWBA: 29 CFR Part 2590 HCFA: 45 CFR Parts 144, 146 and 148
August 20, 1999	Federal Enforcement in Group and Individual Health Insurance Markets; Interim Rule	Details procedures for enforcing Title XXVII of the Public Health Service Act as added by HIPAA and as amended, in states that do not enforce the requirements of these acts. Delineates the process for taking enforcement actions against non-federal government plans, and, in those states in which HCFA (now named CMS) is directly enforcing the requirements, health insurance issuers that are not complying with the requirements.	Comment period ended October 19, 1999	HCFA: 45 CFR Parts 144, 146, 148 and 150
October 25, 1999	Health Insurance Portability; Final Rule	Solicitation of additional comments on interim rules published on April 8, 1997 regarding a number of portability, access and renewability provisions as well as comments reflecting the experience that interested parties have had with the interim regulations. Also clarifies definition of late enrollee for purposes of applying pre-existing exclusion period.	Comment period ended January 25, 2000	IRS: 26 CFR Part 54 PWBA: 29 CFR Part 25 90 HCFA: 45 CFR Subtitle A, Parts 144 and 146
January 8, 2001	Nondiscrimination in Health Coverage in the Group Market; Interim Final Rules and Proposed Rules	Interim rules regarding provisions prohibiting discrimination based on a health factor for group health plans and issuers of health insurance coverage in connection with a group health plans. Proposed standards for defining bona fide wellness programs.	Comment period ended April 9, 2001	IRS: 26 CFR Part 54 PWBA: 29 CFR Part 2590 HCFA: 45 CFR Part 146
March 9, 2001	Interim Final Rules for Nondiscrimination in Health Coverage in the Group Market	Delays for 60 days, the effective dates for the nondiscrimination rule published on January 8, 2001	Final	IRS: 26 CFR Part 54 PWBA: 29 CFR Part 2590 HCFA: 45 CFR Part 146

Source: Congressional Research Service

Does HIPAA make any Changes in COBRA Continuation of Coverage Requirements?

Yes, the Act makes several changes to the laws providing for COBRA continuation of coverage. It provides:

- a clarification that a disabled qualified beneficiary and all other qualified family members of the beneficiary are also eligible for the additional 11 months of COBRA;

- that the qualifying event of disability applies in the case of a qualified beneficiary who is determined under the Social Security Act to be disabled during the first 60 days of COBRA coverage;

- that a qualified beneficiary for COBRA coverage includes a child who is born to, or placed for adoption with, the covered employee during the period of COBRA coverage; and

- that COBRA can be terminated if a qualified beneficiary becomes covered under a group health plan which does not contain any exclusion or limitation affecting a participant or his or her beneficiaries because of the requirements of the Act.

It should also be noted that under the Medical Savings Account (MSA) provisions of the Act (see below), individuals may withdraw funds from their MSAs without penalty to pay their COBRA premiums.

PART III. OTHER PROVISIONS

In addition to the insurance provisions discussed above, HIPAA includes other provisions affecting health care. This section briefly summarizes these provisions.[29]

---

[29] Not included in this summary are HIPAA provisions that were revenue raisers; these related to company-owned life insurance, individuals who lose U.S. citizenship or who were long-term residents and terminate U.S. residency, and interest allocation rules for financial institutions.

Administrative Simplification

In addition to provisions relating to private health insurance, HIPAA directed the Secretary of HHS to issue standards to support and promote the electronic transmission of health care information between payers and providers. The standards specify the content and format of electronic health care claims and other common administrative and financial health care transactions (e.g., health plan enrollment, referrals). They are intended to streamline administrative operations within the health care system, which currently stores and transmits health information in numerous paper and electronic formats. HIPAA's administrative simplification provisions also instructed the Secretary of HHS to develop security standards and safeguards, which health plans and providers must incorporate into their operations to protect health information from unauthorized access, use, and disclosure. Finally, the Secretary was directed to develop standards for unique identifiers (i.e., ID numbers) for patients, employers, health plans, and providers.

The growing use of information technology in the management, administration, and delivery of health care has led to increasing public concern over the privacy of medical information. Patients are worried about who has access to their medical records without their express authorization. They fear that their personal health information will be used against them to deny insurance, employment, and housing, or to expose them to unwanted judgment and scrutiny. Lawmakers addressed these concerns by including in HIPAA's administrative simplification provisions a timetable for developing standards to protect the privacy of health information. HIPAA gave Congress until August 21, 1999, to enact comprehensive health privacy legislation, otherwise the Secretary was instructed to develop privacy standards. Congress was unable to meet its own deadline and so the Secretary proceeded to develop a health information privacy rule. The final rule was issued on December 28, 2000, and modifications to the rule were published on August 14, 2002. The compliance deadline for most covered entities is April 14, 2003.

Medical Savings Accounts

HIPAA authorized tax-advantaged medical savings accounts (MSAs) under a demonstration that began in 1997.[30] MSAs (now formally called Archer MSAs) are personal savings accounts for unreimbursed medical expenses. They can be used to pay for health care not covered by insurance, including deductibles and copayments. Currently, a limited number of MSAs may be established by taxpayers who have qualifying high deductible insurance (and none other, with some exceptions) and who either are self-employed or are employees covered by the high deductible plan established by their small employer.

Employer contributions to MSAs are not subject to either income or employment taxes, while contributions made by individuals - allowed only if the employer does not contribute - are allowed as an above-the-line deduction (not limited to itemizers). MSAs are held in trust by insurance companies, banks, and other financial institutions, and whatever earnings they have are exempt from taxes. Withdrawals are not taxed if they are for medical expenses unreimbursed by insurance or otherwise, while other distributions, being non-qualified, are included in gross income and subject with some exceptions to an additional 15% penalty.

The IRS has estimated that 62,232 MSAs received contributions in tax year 2000 and that an additional 22,640 were established prior to July 1, 2001; the total is far lower than the 750,000 statutory ceiling.[31] The slow growth can be attributed to a number of factors including product familiarity, consumer aversion to financial risk, and the reluctance of insurance agents to sell lower-priced policies; however, statutory restrictions undoubtedly have played some role.

Health Insurance for Self-Employed Taxpayers

HIPAA increased the portion of premiums that self-employed taxpayers may deduct from income for the purposes of determining federal taxes owed. Under prior law the deduction was 30% of health insurance costs; HIPAA

---

[30] Under HIPAA, no new MSAs (with some exceptions) were to be established after December 31, 2000; the cut-off would have been earlier had thresholds on the number of accounts been exceeded. P.L. 106-554 extended the deadline for new accounts to December 31, 2002.

[31] IRS Announcement 2000-99, October, 2001. MSAs are not counted toward the statutory ceiling if the owners were previously uninsured; moreover, all accounts established by an individual are added together and married individuals opening separate accounts are treated as having one account.

increased it to 40% in 1997; 45% in 1998 through 2002; 50% in 2003; 60% in 2004; 70% in 2005; and 80% in 2006 and thereafter. Subsequent legislation (P.L. 105-34 and P.L. 105-277) accelerated and increased the percentages set by HIPAA. Today the deduction is set at 70% in 2002, and will rise to 100% in 2003 and thereafter. As discussed in the following section, the legislation also allowed self-employed taxpayers to take account of long-term care insurance premiums in making this deduction.

In addition, HIPAA provided that payments for personal injury or sickness through an arrangement having the effect of accident or health insurance are excluded from gross income (that is, they are exempt from taxation), provided the arrangement has adequate risk shifting and is not merely a reimbursement arrangement. Thus with respect to taxes, payments from self-insured plans covering self-employed individuals are treated like payments from commercial insurance.

Long-Term Care

HIPAA established new rules regarding the tax treatment of long-term care insurance and expenses, effective January 1, 1997. Qualified long-term care insurance is treated as accident and health insurance, and benefits are treated as amounts received for personal injuries and sickness and reimbursement for medical expenses actually incurred. As a consequence, benefits are excluded from gross income (that is, exempt from taxation). The exclusion for benefits paid on a per diem or other periodic basis is limited to the greater of (1) $220 a day (in 2003) or (2) the cost of long-term care services.[32]

Employer contributions to the cost of qualified long-term care insurance premiums are excluded from the gross income of the employee. The exclusion does not apply to insurance provided through employer-sponsored cafeteria plans or flexible spending accounts.

Unreimbursed long-term care expenses are allowed as itemized deductions to the extent they and other unreimbursed medical expenses exceed 7.5% of adjusted gross income. Long-term care insurance premiums can be counted as these expenses subject to age-adjusted limits. In 2003,

---

[32] Treating long-term care insurance as accident and health insurance and excluding benefits from gross income also exempts the inside buildup of the insurance from taxation. Long-term care insurance usually has premiums that do not increase with age (aside from optional inflation adjustments for some policies); premiums for early years of a policy and the earnings on them (the inside buildup) help pay for costs later on. The tax treatment of *nonqualified* long-term care insurance remains uncertain.7

these limits range from $250 for persons age 40 or less to $3,130 for persons over age 70.

Self-employed individuals are allowed to include long-term care insurance premiums in determining their above-the-line deduction (not limited to itemizers) for health insurance expenses. Only amounts not exceeding the age-adjusted limits can be included. As described in the previous section, this deduction is limited to 60% in 1999 through 2001, 70% in 2002, and 100% in 2003 and thereafter.

Qualified long-term care insurance is defined as a contract that covers only long-term care services; does not pay or reimburse expenses covered under Medicare; is guaranteed renewable; does not provide for a cash surrender value or other money that can be paid, assigned, or pledged as collateral for a loan, or borrowed; applies all refunds of premiums and all policy holder dividends or similar amounts as a reduction in future premiums or to increase future benefits; and meets certain consumer protection standards. Policies issued before January 1, 1997, and meeting a state's long-term care insurance requirements at the time the policy was issued are considered qualified insurance for purposes of favorable tax treatment.

Qualified long-term care services are defined as necessary diagnostic, preventive, therapeutic, curing, treating, mitigating, and rehabilitative services, and maintenance or personal care services, which are required by a chronically ill individual, and are provided according to a plan of care prescribed by a licensed health care practitioner. However, amounts paid for services provided by the spouse of a chronically ill person or by a relative directly or through a partnership, corporation, or other entity will not be considered a medical expense eligible for favorable tax treatment, unless the service is provided by a licensed professional.

Chronically ill persons are defined as those individuals:

- unable to perform without substantial assistance from another individual at least two of the following activities of daily living (ADLs) for a period of at least 90 days due to a loss of functional capacity: bathing, dressing, transferring, toileting, eating, and continence;[33]

- having a level of disability similar to the level of disability specified for functional impairments (as determined by the Secretary of the

---

[33] A qualified long-term care insurance contract must take into account at least five of these six activities.

Treasury in consultation with the Secretary of Health and Human Services); or

- requiring substantial supervision to protect them from threats to health and safety due to severe cognitive impairment.

HIPAA required that a licensed health practitioner (physician, registered professional nurse, licensed social worker, or other individual prescribed by the Secretary of the Treasury) certify that a person meets these criteria within the preceding 12-month period.

Accelerated Death Benefits

HIPAA clarified that accelerated death benefits (that is, benefits paid before death) received under a life insurance contract on the life of an insured terminally or chronically ill individual are excluded from gross income. Also excluded are amounts received from a viatical settlement provider for the sale or assignment of a life insurance contract.[34] These exclusions do not apply to amounts paid to persons other than the insured if they have an insurable interest in the insured for business reasons.

A terminally ill individual is one who has been certified by a physician as having an illness or physical condition which can reasonably be expected to result in death within 24 months of the date of certification.

A chronically ill individual is defined the same way as for long-term care (see the previous section). In this case, the exclusion of accelerated death benefits is limited to the actual costs of long-term care incurred by the individual that are not compensated by insurance or otherwise. The exclusion for benefits paid on a per diem or other periodic basis is limited to the greater of (1) $200 a day (in 2001) or (2) the costs of long-term care services.[35] Contracts must not pay or reimburse expenses which are reimbursable under Medicare or would be but for the application of a deductible or coinsurance amount. In addition, contracts are subject to the consumer protection provisions specified in the tax code for long-term care insurance, except for analogous standards specifically applying to

---

[34] Viatical settlement providers must be regularly engaged in the business of purchasing or accepting assignment of life insurance contracts on the lives of terminally or chronically ill individuals. They must be licensed in the state where the insured individual resides or meet certain National Association of Insurance Commissioners standards.

[35] Excess per diem or other regular payments are not taken into account if the individual has been certified as terminally ill.

chronically ill individuals that are adopted by the National Association of Insurance Commissioners or the state in which the policyholder resides.

State Insurance Pools

HIPAA added two types of organizations to the list of those expressly exempt from the federal income tax: (1) state-sponsored membership organizations that provide insurance coverage or medical care to high-risk individuals, and (2) state-sponsored workmen's compensation reinsurance organizations. Organizations in either classification must meet a number of requirements.

Treatment of Certain Health Insurance Providers

HIPAA allowed health insurance providers (other than health maintenance organizations) that are organized and governed under state laws specifically and exclusively applying to not-for-profit health insurance or service organizations to deduct 25% of claims and expenses incurred during the year, less adjusted surplus. Previously this tax treatment applied only to Blue Cross and Blue Shield organizations.

IRA Distributions for Medical Expenses and Insurance

HIPAA provided that the 10% early withdrawal penalty would no longer apply to individual retirement account (IRA) distributions used to pay medical expenses in excess of 7.5% of adjusted gross income. In addition, it provided that the penalty would not apply to IRA distributions used to pay health insurance premiums after separation from employment in the case of an individual who receives 12 consecutive weeks of unemployment compensation.

Organ and Tissue Donation Information

HIPAA required the Secretary of the Treasury to include organ and tissue donor information, to the extent practicable, in the mailing of individual income tax refunds from February 1, 1997 through June 30, 1997.

Chapter 3

HEALTH INFORMATION STANDARDS, PRIVACY, AND SECURITY: HIPAA'S ADMINISTRATIVE SIMPLIFICATION REGULATIONS[*]

C. Stephen Redhead

INTRODUCTION

The Administrative Simplification provisions of the Health Insurance Portability and Accountability Act of 1996 (HIPAA, P.L. 104-191, 42 U.S.C. 1320d) instructed the Secretary of Health and Human Services (HHS) to develop standards to support electronic data interchange for a variety of administrative and financial health care transactions. The intent of the legislation is to improve health care system efficiency and effectiveness, make it easier to detect fraud and abuse, facilitate access to health and medical information by researchers, and reduce administrative costs.

HIPAA's Administrative Simplification provisions required the Secretary to issue regulations to establish standard electronic formats for billing and other common transactions, including the use of uniform data codes for reporting diagnoses, referrals, authorizations, and medical

---

[*] Excerpted from CRS Report RL30620.

procedures. The legislation also mandated the development of unique identifiers (i.e., ID numbers) for patients, employers, health plans, and health care providers. In addition, HIPAA required the Secretary to issue security standards, including an electronic signature standard, to safeguard confidential health information against unauthorized access, use, and disclosure. Finally, the legislation included a timetable for Congress and the Secretary to develop comprehensive medical records privacy standards to give patients the right to access their health information and control of use and disclosure of such information by others.

The Administrative Simplification provisions cover health plans, health care clearinghouses (i.e., entities that facilitate and process the flow of information between providers and payers), and health care providers who transmit health information electronically. Covered entities have up to 24 months to comply with the standards established by the regulations. Small health plans with annual receipts of $5 million or less have an additional 12 months to comply. Although HIPAA does not mandate electronic transmission of health information, the standards are intended to catalyze the health care industry's gradual shift away from paper-based medical records and transactions to electronic record keeping and data transmission. **Table 1** provides a summary of all the Administrative Simplification provisions in HIPAA, including civil penalties for failure to comply with the standards, and criminal penalties for wrongful disclosure of personally identifiable health information.

This chapter is divided into two sections. The first section provides some background on electronic health information security and privacy. The second section describes each of the HIPAA Administrative Simplification standards, including the status of their implementation. To date, HHS has issued two final rules: electronic transactions and code sets; and privacy. The agency has also proposed standards for security and electronic signatures, and for unique employer and provider identifiers. There is an expanded discussion of the privacy rule, which has generated a great deal of public debate and congressional interest.

ELECTRONIC INTERCHANGE OF HEALTH CARE INFORMATION

Uses and Transmission of Health Information

The U.S. health care industry is made up of more than 12 million providers, payers, researchers, and suppliers in more than 500,000 companies, nonprofit organizations, and research facilities. The transition from fee-for-service health care to managed health care has fueled enormous growth in the demand for patient data by an increasing number of entities. The development of integrated health care delivery systems has, in turn, led to the development of large, integrated databases of personal health information. With access to these data, people are seeking new and improved ways to deliver effective care, identify and treat those at risk for disease, conduct research, assess and improve quality, detect fraud and abuse, and market their services (see text box on following page).

However, today's health care system is still largely paper-based and unstandardized. By some estimates, paperwork alone accounts for more than 20% of all health care costs. In addition, health care providers spend a significant amount of their time filling out forms rather than attending to additional patients. Routine tasks, such as filing a claim for payment from an insurer, checking insurance eligibility for a particular treatment, or responding to requests for additional information to support a claim, can involve numerous paper forms and telephone calls. Physicians often bill multiple health plans, each of which may use a different format for its claims forms. Paper-based medical records confine medical history to one physical location, which may limit patients' ability to share their medical information with other physicians and specialists in order to receive the best possible diagnosis and treatment.

The nation's health insurance payers have employed an enormous variety of formats and data requirements to handle claims and other transactions. Competing parties have developed proprietary formats for electronic data interchange, but there is no uniform set of standards.[1] Under HIPAA, HHS has mandated the adoption of standardized electronic formats for several common health care transactions (e.g., health plan enrollment, health insurance claims, payment and remittance), and the use of five medical data code sets for encoding data elements in those transactions. The industry estimates that full implementation of the transactions standards could yield a net savings of up to $9 billion a year by reducing administrative overhead, while at the same time helping improve the quality of health care by freeing up resources now devoted to paperwork and administration. Adoption of the HIPAA-mandated electronic transactions and codes standards is also likely to increase substantially the use of

---

[1] HHS estimates that there are about 400 formats for electronic health care claims currently in use in the United States.

electronic data interchange (EDI) in health care and help move the country towards the eventual replacement of paper-based transactions with EDI. Details on the status of the standards for electronic transactions, code sets, and unique identifiers appear later in the chapter.

Growing Uses of Health Care Information

Primary users of health care information include physicians, clinics, and hospitals that provide care to patients. Patients provide background medical information to their physicians, who use it to develop treatment plans and order diagnostic tests. Physicians maintain detailed records of medical services provided to patients. Hospitals and clinics use health care information to provide patient care ordered by physicians and maintain ongoing records of medical services provided. In order to be reimbursed by health insurers, health care providers submit claims that often include detailed information about a patient's diagnosis, treatment, and prognosis.

Secondary users of health care information include organizations that pay for health care benefits, such as traditional fee-for-service health insurance companies, managed care providers, and government programs, like Medicare and Medicaid. These health care payers also use health care information to analyze the cost and quality of health care delivered by providers, and to prevent fraud and abuse. Other secondary users of health information include medical and social science researchers, employers, and public health services, who use the information for purposes such as researching the costs and benefits of alternative medical interventions, determining eligibility for social programs, and understanding state and local health care needs. Much of the health data available to secondary users specifically identifies individual patients.

The expansion of managed care has stimulated a demand for patient data that could barely be imagined a decade ago. Managed care organizations (MCOs) operate on the principle that by monitoring and controlling patient care, they can deliver care more efficiently and reduce costs. To achieve these objectives, many different groups employed by or under contract to MCOs must analyze patient data for a wide variety or purposes, including utilization review (How are participating providers using services?) risk management (Is the MCO at legal or financial risk?), and quality assessment (How can patient care and outcomes be improved?).

Health Information Security

There has always been a need to protect confidential medical information against unauthorized access and disclosure. For paper records, physical protections such as locks, safes, and controlled-access buildings often provided adequate security. In addition, the time and effort required to copy extensive health records and transport them from one location to another effectively discouraged widespread dissemination and disclosure of health information. But those safeguards may also impede the delivery of quality patient care, because important information is not always available when and where it is needed. While electronic data interchange holds great promise for improving health care delivery, it also raises serious security concerns. Digital records may easily be copied, modified, or viewed remotely by people seeking to misuse the information. Health information that used to be protected by physical means can now be copied and transmitted across the country with the click of a mouse.

Information technology experts estimate that more than 120 e-Health companies were created in 1999. They predict that within a few years we will be able to access all our medical information online from our homes and offices. Routine tasks such as selecting physicians, identifying medical care options, viewing medical test results, and scheduling appointments will be conducted over the Internet. Hospitals, physicians, and health insurance companies will also conduct business over the Internet. However, the health care industry lags behind other industries (e.g., financial services) in implementing security technologies to protect electronic health information. Without appropriate security processes and technologies in place, security threats to electronic health information are likely to increase dramatically.

There are many different components that are required to establish and maintain information security both in the paper world and the digital world. For any domain, there must be an authority that creates an identity for itself and issues identities at lower levels. For example, a private company may issue employee identity cards that enable access to facilities, benefits, or systems within the company. Those identities would not be valid at a government facility because the private company has no authority outside its own domain. Identities issued by authorities are part of the authentication process, by which individuals are positively identified in order to gain access to information systems. An identity is only valid if the person or system that is authenticating it recognizes the authority of the issuing body.

Signed paper documents and identification cards, such as a driver's license, are often used to verify a person's identity. People trust a driver's license because they are aware of the steps required to obtain one and they recognize that there are controls in place to protect against modification and forgery. Authentication is more difficult in the digital world, because information can be more easily obtained, copied, and modified. User passwords are a common form of authentication used by digital information systems, but they are easy to obtain and exploit. Digital signatures (discussed below) and biometrics (i.e., use of unique physical attributes such as fingerprints, or retina patterns), though more expensive and difficult to implement, provide a very high degree of authentication. Once a user's identity has been authenticated, that individual may then receive authorization to access, modify, create, or delete information within a system.

Confidentiality and Cryptography

In digital information systems, confidentiality can be achieved through the use of cryptography (i.e., disguising a message with code). To send a message via insecure channels, the message is encoded, or encrypted, using a cryptographic formula called an encryption key. The resulting encrypted message can only be unscrambled, or decrypted, using a decryption key, which is either the same as the encryption key or mathematically related to it. With cryptography, any kind of digital information — text, data, voice, images — can be encrypted. There are two types of cryptography.

In **secret key cryptography**, the key used by the sender to encrypt the message is also used by the recipient to decrypt the message. Both parties must therefore arrange to share the same key. If the key has to be transmitted from the sender to the recipient, both parties must ensure that the transmission system is secure so that the key cannot be intercepted.

In **public key cryptography**, each person gets a pair of keys, a private key and a public key. The private key is kept secure, known only to the user, while the public key is published in the electronic equivalent of a telephone book. To use this kind of system, the sender encrypts the message using the recipient's public key. The message can only be decrypted by the recipient using her private key. Public key cryptography thus permits the secure transmission of information across open networks, such as the Internet, without senders and recipients having to exchange secret keys.

Public key cryptography requires an infrastructure (Public Key Infrastructure, or PKI) to support the information technology applications and manage the generation, certification, and distribution of public and private keys.

While encryption ensures confidentiality, it does not by itself guarantee data integrity and non-repudiation. Integrity is the assurance that a message remains unaltered during transit and storage. For example, sealing an envelope provides some guarantee of integrity for paper documents. Non-repudiation is the guarantee that a particular transmission actually occurred, and that neither the sender nor the receiver are able to deny it. In the digital world, integrity and non-repudiation are accomplished through the use of digital signatures.

Digital Signatures

A digital signature is a type of electronic signature that is attached to an electronic document to provide authentication of the signer's identity, much like a handwritten signature on a printed document. The recipient of a document with a digital signature is able to verify that the document did indeed originate from the person whose signature is attached (i.e., sender authentication) and that the document has not been altered since it was signed (i.e., data integrity). Moreover, digital signatures cannot be repudiated, that is, the signer of a document cannot later disown it by claiming it was forged (i.e., non-repudiation). The use of digital signatures grew out of the development of public key cryptography (see text box on the following page). Digital signatures are an important component of information security systems and their use, though not widespread, is growing rapidly.

HIPAA's Administrative Simplification provisions instructed the Secretary to issue security standards to ensure the integrity and confidentiality of electronic health information, and to protect such information against unauthorized use and disclosure. The law also required the Secretary to develop an electronic signature standard. The provisions and implementation status of the proposed security and electronic signature rule are summarized below.

Health Information Privacy

The growing use of information technology in the management, administration, and delivery of health care has led to increasing public concern over the privacy of medical information. Polls indicate that people are worried about who has access to their medical records without their express authorization. They fear that their personal health information will be used against them to deny insurance, employment, and housing, or to expose them to unwanted judgment and scrutiny.[2]

What is a Digital Signature?

A digital signature is a method of authenticating electronic documents that combines the use of public key cryptography with mathematical algorithms known as hash functions. When you apply a hash function to a document, it creates a concise digital fingerprint of the document called a message digest. The message digest is of fixed length, regardless of the length of the original document. Hash functions are designed so that a small change in the document produces a large change in the resulting message digest. Once you have created a message digest from a document, you cannot re-create the document from the digest.

To create a digital signature, the sender first passes the document through a hash function to produce a message digest. The sender then encrypts the message digest using her private key. The result is a digital signature, which is appended to the original document (which the sender may also encrypt using her private key). The document is then transmitted to the intended recipient, who decrypts the digital signature using the sender's public key to change it back into a message digest. The recipient creates a second message digest by passing the document through the same hash function as used by the sender.

The recipient then compares the two digests. If they are identical, the recipient can be sure that the document was not altered during transmission. Because the sender is the only individual with access to the private key used to encrypt the digest, the recipient is also assured that the information has indeed been sent by the sender, who is unable to deny that fact. Although the entire process sounds complicated, in practice it requires little more than selecting an icon on a computer screen.

Information privacy, as distinct from information security, may be defined as the right of individuals to determine when, how, and to what extent they will share personal information about themselves with others. Use and disclosure of anonymized information, from which all personal identifiers have been removed, is generally not considered to compromise privacy. The degree of privacy protection afforded to personal medical

---

[2] A national survey conducted by Princeton Survey Research Associations and released in January 1999 found that one in five people believe that their personal health information has been used inappropriately, without their knowledge or consent.

information provided to a physician or health insurance company by a patient varies from state to state. There is no comprehensive federal law that protects the privacy of medical information.[3]

Advocates of strong privacy protection insist that patients be given the ability to deny access to their medical information to virtually any third party. They also seek to prohibit health care plans and providers from requiring patients to waive those rights as a condition of participation in the health care system. But health plans, researchers, pharmaceutical companies, and others argue that too much privacy (i.e., strict patient consent requirements for the release of personally identifiable health information) may suppress the flow of information and stifle efforts to improve the quality and efficiency of health care.

The implied conflict between patient privacy protection and the promotion of health care quality and efficiency may be an exaggeration. There is growing evidence from polls and surveys that some people are withdrawing from full participation in their own health care because they are afraid their health records will be disclosed to employers and others and lead to discrimination, loss of benefits, stigma, or unwanted exposure. A January 1999 survey by the California Health Care Foundation found that one of every six people engaged in some form of privacy-protective behavior, including lying to their doctor, refusing to provide information or providing inaccurate information, doctor-hopping to avoid a consolidated medical record, paying out-of-pocket for care that is covered by insurance, or avoiding care altogether. As a result, patients risk inadequate medical care, and the data disclosed and used for payment, outcomes analysis, research, and public health reporting are compromised. Thus, some advocates argue that strong privacy protection goes hand-in-hand with promoting health care quality, access, and efficiency.

House and Senate conferees added privacy language to the Administrative Simplification provisions of HIPAA during the bill's conference, after lawmakers had failed to pass stand-alone health privacy legislation. HIPAA required the Secretary to report to Congress by August 1997 on ways to protect the privacy of personally identifiable health information. It then gave Congress until August 21, 1999 to enact health privacy legislation. If Congress failed to act, then the Secretary was instructed to issue health privacy regulations by February 21, 2000.

---

[3] The Privacy Act of 1974 (5 U.S.C. 552a) protects personally identifiable information collected and held by federal agencies. Federal law also provides substantial privacy protection for people who receive drug and alcohol treatment at federally funded clinics (42 U.S.C. 290dd-2). Several other statutes provide limited protection under specific circumstances.

The Secretary presented her recommendations on health privacy legislation to Congress on September 11, 1997, at a hearing before the Senate Committee on Labor and Human Resources.[4] The recommendations were intended to serve as guidance to Congress in developing comprehensive privacy legislation. The Secretary outlined the following five key principles as being fundamental to the protection of personally identifiable health information:

- Boundaries: Limit, with few exceptions, the use of an individual's health information to health purposes only.

- Security: Require organizations that handle health information to provide adequate security against unauthorized access, disclosure, and misuse.

- Consumer Control: Provide patients with the right to inspect, copy, and, if necessary, correct their health information, and provide patients with details of who has access to their information, how that information will be used, and how they can restrict or limit access to it.

- Accountability: Penalize those who misuse health information and provide redress for those harmed by improper use and disclosure.

- Public Responsibility: Balance privacy protections with public responsibility to support national priorities, including public health and safety, research, and law enforcement.

Several health privacy bills were introduced during 1999, but lawmakers were unable to meet the HIPAA-imposed deadline for enacting comprehensive health privacy legislation.[5] In June 1999, the Senate Committee on Health, Education, Labor, and Pensions delayed indefinitely an attempt to mark up a health privacy bill after lawmakers failed to agree on whether to give patients the right to sue over breaches of medical record confidentiality, and whether to allow preemption of all state health privacy laws. With the failure of Congress to meet its self-imposed deadline, the

---

[4] The Secretary's report on the confidentiality of personally identifiable health information is available online at [http://aspe.os.dhhs.gov/admnsimp/pvcrec.htm].

[5] The following health privacy bills were introduced in the 106th Congress: S. 573 (Leahy), S. 578 (Jeffords), S. 881 (Bennett), H.R. 1057 (Markey, identical to S. 573), H.R. 1941 (Condit), H.R. 2404 (Murtha), H.R. 2455 (Shays), and H.R. 2470 (Greenwood).

Secretary proceeded to develop health privacy regulations based on the five principles outlined in her report to Congress.

HHS issued a proposed rule on November 3, 1999. At the request of several health care groups, the 60-day public comment period was extended by an additional 45 days, during which time the agency received more than 52,000 comments. Numerous stakeholders provided extensive comments on the proposed rule, including patient privacy advocates, health care providers, standards and accrediting organizations, government entities, health care clearinghouses, employers, health plans, and research and pharmaceutical groups. HHS issued a final health privacy rule on December 28, 2000. An overview of the rule's provisions and a discussion of some of the key concerns and issues raised by stakeholders is provided below.

HIPAA'S ADMINISTRATIVE SIMPLIFICATION STANDARDS

Electronic Transactions and Code Sets

On August 17, 2000, HHS published a final rule to implement standards for electronic health care transactions.[6] The standards are intended to reduce the administrative burden on health plans and health care providers, which today exchange information using many different paper and electronic formats. Each standard specifies the content and format of a common administrative or financial transaction between health plans and health care providers. The eight transactions covered under the rule are: health care claims; eligibility for health care; referral certification and authorization; health care claim status; enrollment and disenrollment in a health plan; health care payment and remittance advice; health plan premium payments; and coordination of benefits.[7] The rule defines the specific standard to be used for each transaction, the standard-setting organization whose standard must be used, and where implementation specifications can be obtained.

---

[6] 65 *Federal Register* 50311–50373.

[7] HIPAA required the Secretary to adopt standards for two additional transactions: first report of injury, and health claims attachments (i.e., extra documentation, such as operative notes, pathology reports, or medical history, used to support or supplement a request for payment). The first report of injury standard was not finalized because an implementation guide was not available in time. HIPAA gave the Secretary an extra 12 months to issue a claims attachments standard.

HIPAA required the Secretary, where possible, to adopt standards developed by private standards development organizations (SDOs), which are accredited by the American National Standards Institute (ANSI). HHS chose to use standards developed by the Accredited Standards Committee (ASC) X12N, except for the standards for retail pharmacy transactions, which are from the National Council for Prescription Drug Programs (NCPDP).[8] Both sets of standards are already in widespread use.

All health plans (except for self-administered, employer-sponsored plans serving fewer than 50 employees) and health care clearinghouses, and all health care providers that choose to submit or receive a HIPAA-covered transaction are required to use these standards. Neither HIPAA nor the final rule requires physicians or other providers to submit transactions electronically. However, if they submit a HIPAA covered transaction electronically, it must comply with the standard specified in the rule. Health care clearinghouses may accept non-standard transactions for the sole purpose of translating them into standard transactions for sending providers, and may accept standard transactions and translate them into non-standard transactions for receiving providers.

The rule names six organizations that have agreed to serve as Designated Standards Maintenance Organizations (DSMOs).[9] These organizations will evaluate requests for changes to the standards and make recommendations for the Secretary's consideration. Under HIPAA, the Secretary may modify a standard no more frequently than once every 12 months.

In addition to the standards for electronic transactions, the rule adopts several widely used code sets for encoding data elements in the transactions. Medical data code sets include diagnostic codes and medical procedure codes. The code sets adopted under the rule are:

- International Classification of Diseases, 9th Edition, Clinical Modification, (ICD-9-CM), Volumes 1 and 2, for diagnosing diseases, injuries, impairments and other health problems, and identifying their causes.

---

[8] ACS X12 was chartered by ANSI in 1979 to develop and promote standards to facilitate the electronic exchange of data. The "N" denotes the insurance subcommittee.

[9] The six DSMOs are: Accredited Standards Committee X12; Dental Content Committee; Health Level Seven; National Council for Prescription Drug Programs; National Uniform Billing Committee; and National Uniform Claims Committee.

- International Classification of Diseases, 9th Edition, Clinical Modification, (ICD-9-CM), Volume 3, for reporting inpatient medical procedures by hospitals.
- Current Procedural Terminology, 4th Edition, (CPT-4), and Health Care Financing Administration Procedure Coding System (HCPCS), Level 1, for reporting physician services and other health care services (e.g., radiological procedures, clinical diagnostic tests, hearing and vision services).
- Health Care Financing Administration Procedure Coding System (HCPCS), Level 2, for reporting all other substances, equipment, supplies, or other items used in health care services (e.g., medical supplies, orthotic and prosthetic devices, durable medical equipment).
- Code on Dental Procedures and Nomenclature, 2nd Edition, for reporting dental services.
- National Drug Codes (NDC) for reporting prescription drugs and biologics.

The rule eliminates the use of local HCPCS codes (i.e., Level 3), which state Medicaid programs and other health insurers have developed to identify many of the services for which they pay. Public and private insurers may submit local codes to HCFA for review and inclusion in the appropriate national code set. Local codes generally fall into one of three categories. The first category includes local codes that are basically the same as existing national codes that describe services commonly provided by other payers. These local codes are sometimes used to facilitate special payment arrangements with certain providers. Secondly, there are local codes that reflect services, including new and emerging technologies (e.g., telemedicine), that are covered by state Medicaid programs and other payers, for which no national code currently exists. Finally, many local codes are used to describe special or unique services covered by a state Medicaid program, but not generally covered by other health insurers. For example, Medicaid Home and Community-Based Waiver programs may cover a wide range of non-medical services such as case management, homemaker services, respite care, and transportation.

In November 1999, the National Association of State Medicaid Directors established the National Medicaid EDI HIPAA (NMEH) Workgroup to assess the impact of HIPAA's Administrative Simplification standards on state Medicaid programs. Using a 49-state database of local codes, workgroup participants have prepared a consolidated and prioritized list of a few thousand codes to submit to the HCFA HCPCS Committee. Medicaid officials question whether HCFA currently has the resources to process such a large submission in a timely manner. They are concerned that states will have to continue to use local codes beyond the compliance deadline.

The electronic transactions and code sets rule took effect on October 16, 2000. Covered entities have 2 years to come into compliance (i.e., October 16, 2002). Small health plans with a maximum of $5 million in annual receipts have an additional year to comply (see **Table 2**). HCFA estimates that the rule will provide a net savings to the health care industry of $29.9 billion over 10 years.

National Provider Identifier

HHS proposed standards for a national health care provider identifier on May 7, 1998.[10] Under the proposal, each provider would be required to use a unique eight-character, alphanumeric identifier on all health care transactions, including electronic ones.[11] The identifier would contain no embedded intelligence (i.e., no information about the provider). At present, health plans assign identification numbers to health care providers. Providers that do business with multiple health plans often have multiple identification numbers, which can slow administrative activities and increase costs.

National provider identifiers would be issued by the National Provider System (NPS), based on information entered into the NPS by one or more organizations known as enumerators. HHS asked for comment on whether a federally directed registry should act at the sole enumerator of all health care providers nationwide, or whether a combination of federal and state entities should act as enumerators. HHS received and reviewed about 5000 public comments on its proposal and expects to issue a final rule later this year (see **Table 2**).

---

[10] 63 *Federal Register* 25320–25357.
[11] Many commenters on the proposed rule preferred a 10-digit numeric identifier with a check digit in the last position to help detect keying error.

National Health Plan Identifier

A Notice of Proposed Rulemaking (NPRM) for the national health plan identifier is under development at HHS and is expected to be published later this year (see **Table 2**).

National Employer Identifier

In a June 16, 1998 NPRM, HHS proposed adopting the Employer Identification Number (EIN) to identify employers in all health care transactions.[12] The EIN is a nine-digit taxpayer identification number for employers that is assigned by the Internal Revenue Service. Unlike the social security number, the EIN does not contain any embedded information and is not considered confidential. EINs are freely exchanged by employers and others. HHS received and reviewed about 800 public comments on the employer identifier NPRM. The agency expects to issue a final rule later this year (see **Table 2**).

National Individual Identifier

In contrast to the public's general acceptance of the health information standards discussed above, public opinion on the unique individual identifier is deeply divided. On July 31, 1998, in response to widespread public concern, then Vice President Gore announced that the Administration would not develop a unique individual identifier until health privacy protections were in place. Lawmakers also introduced legislation during the 105th Congress to repeal the HIPAA requirement for HHS to adopt standards for a unique individual identifier, but the bills died in committee without hearings.[13] Congress included a provision in the FY1999 Omnibus Appropriations Act (P.L. 105-277) that prohibited HHS from developing a unique individual identifier standard until legislation is enacted specifically approving the standard. The same provision appeared in the FY2000 Consolidated Appropriations Act (P.L. 106-113) and again in the FY2001 Consolidated Appropriations Act (P.L. 106-554).[14]

---

[12] 63 *Federal Register* 32784–32798.
[13] (i) H.R. 4312 (Barr), Medical Privacy Protection Act of 1998; (ii) S. 2352 (Leahy), Patient Privacy Rights Act of 1998.
[14] The provision was Section 516 of the FY1999 Labor/HHS/Education Appropriations Act, and Section 514 in both the FY2000 and FY2001 Labor/HHS/Education Appropriations Act.

HIPAA recognized the unique identifier for individuals as an essential component of administrative simplification. Evidence suggests that the use of a unique individual identifier would improve the quality of health care and reduce administrative costs. Today, organizations and individuals involved in health care, including health insurance companies, health plans, managed care organizations, clinics, hospitals, physicians, and pharmacies, frequently assign identifiers to individuals for use within their systems. Those identifiers often vary among organizations, so it is not uncommon for providers and plans to use different identifiers for the same patient. Having multiple identifiers for the same individual within or across organizations may prevent or inhibit timely access to integrated information. There is substantial support within the health industry for the adoption of a unique identifier for individuals, provided there are appropriate protections against misuse and unauthorized use outside of health care.

Controversy over the adoption of a standard for a unique individual identifier has largely focused on privacy concerns. Opponents of a unique individual identifier argue that its use could facilitate access to personal information by unscrupulous employers and insurers, who might then use the information to discriminate in hiring and insuring individuals with serious or costly health problems. Proposals to use the social security number as a unique health identifier have been strongly criticized because of the concern that it would make it easier to link medical records with other information about an individual, including financial and employment data. For many advocates, privacy threats outweigh any practical benefits of adopting a unique individual health identifier, such as improved patient care or administrative savings.

In an attempt to address the controversy surrounding the use of a unique health identifier, HHS departed from its customary rulemaking process and decided to solicit information and public input on a variety of options and approaches for individual health identifiers before issuing a proposed standard. The agency released a White Paper discussing those options and planned a series of public hearings by the National Committee on Vital and Health Statistics (NCVHS).[15] The initial NCVHS hearing, which was held in Chicago on July 20-21, 1998, drew significant media attention and sparked widespread public concern, which led to the Administration's announcement that it was putting development of the unique individual identifier on hold until privacy protections were issued. Even though the health privacy rule

---

[15] NCVHS serves as the statutory public advisory body to the Secretary of HHS in the area of health data and statistics [http://www.ncvhs.hhs.gov].

recently took effect (see discussion below), the legislative rider in this year's appropriations bill prohibits HHS from resuming work on developing a unique individual identifier.

Security and Electronic Signature

HHS proposed health information security and electronic signature standards on August 12, 1998.[16] There are no existing standards that integrate all the security components necessary to protect health information confidentiality. Therefore, HHS developed new standards, which define a set of requirements that health care plans, providers, and clearinghouses must include in their operations to ensure that electronic health information remains secure. The proposed rule also describes the implementation features that must be present in order to satisfy each requirement.

The agency received and reviewed more than 2000 public comments on the proposed standards and is expected to issue a final rule in the next few months. Analysts anticipate that the definitions in the final rule will be aligned with those that appeared in the final transactions and privacy rules. They also expect a clarification that the final security rule covers health information transmitted or maintained in any form or medium (including paper records and oral communications), as does the final privacy rule. Beyond that, analysts are not expecting any substantial changes in the final security rule. Prior to the Bush Administration, HHS indicated that it intended to carve out the electronic signature standard and issue it as a separate rule.

Security

The proposed security standards do not mandate specific technologies to be used. HHS opted for a technologically neutral approach so as not to bind the health care community to systems and/or software that may soon be superceded by new products in the rapidly developing field of information security technology. The standards include a compendium of organizational and technical practices and procedures that must be adopted. The proposal is also designed to give health care entities of different size and complexity the flexibility to develop their own particular implementation solutions as long as the basic requirements are met. The proposed security standards include four sets of provisions.

---

[16] 63 *Federal Register* 43241–43280.

Administrative Procedures

Most of HIPAA security compliance will be administrative and operational in nature. The proposed rule requires a security assessment and risk analysis. Policy and procedure requirements include: assigning authorities to individuals assigned to authorize various level of physical access; defining physical and data access levels based on role; employee security orientation; tracking employee access to applications, systems, data, and physical areas; and termination procedures that ensure recovery of keys and access cards, and removal of access to applications, systems, and data.

Physical Safeguards

The proposed rule contains several requirements to protect computers and physical records. They include: facility management; physical access controls; computer room access; medical records access/tracking; shredding policies; and workstation location policies.

Technical Security Services

The technical security services provisions deal with systems and software applications that protect and control access to electronic information. They are designed to ensure that users only have access to those systems, applications, and data for which they are authorized. Technical solutions may be as simple as user passwords or include more complex devices such as biometrics. The proposed rule also requires an audit trail policy to track user access.

Technical Security Mechanisms

These provisions are intended to protect the transmission of patient data over public networks (e.g., Intranet, Internet). They require the appropriate deployment of security software, including Internet use monitoring, encryption, digital signatures, firewalls, and virus protection.

Electronic Signature

HHS proposed adopting digital signatures (with properties that ensure message integrity, non-repudiation, and user authentication) as the electronic signature standard. The standard applies only to HIPAA-specified transactions that employ an electronic signature. It does not mandate the use of electronic signatures. None of the transactions adopted under HIPAA currently require an electronic signature, though they may do so in the future. As previously mentioned, HHS is expected to remove electronic signatures from the final security rule. At the request of the Commerce

Department's National Institute of Standards and Technology (NIST), HHS agreed to defer issuing a final electronic signature standard until an assessment of this evolving technology has been completed.

Standardization and Interoperability of Information Technologies

At a March 2000 hearing before the House Science Subcommittee on Technology, a panel of health care information technology experts urged federal agencies to develop a set of technology standards by which all health care information security systems could be evaluated.[17] Without such standards, health care plans and providers who seek to integrate information technology systems have no way of knowing whether the security components of the products they purchase will perform as expected. By one estimate, there are more than 1600 companies developing and selling health care information technology, with no underlying industry standard security requirements for their products. A wide variety of commercial products are available, including operating systems, database management systems, firewalls, smartcards, network devices, and PKI applications, each with different capabilities and limitations. Without technology standards, consumers may be left wondering how to choose the product that best suits their needs and which provides the appropriate level of security.

The experts also testified that the lack of interoperability among information technology systems presents a barrier to the widespread utilization of electronic information in health care. For example, there is currently no way of ensuring that the system used by one physician will be compatible with that of another physician with whom she plans to share data electronically. The current situation in the health care industry is in stark contrast to the banking industry. Early in the development of the banking industry's information infrastructure, financial institutions saw the value of interoperability that would allow a customer from any bank to execute certain financial transactions from automated teller machines (ATMs) all over the world. Instead of developing proprietary technologies, these companies adhered to uniform standards and sought competitive advantage in other ways.

The National Information Assurance Partnership (NIAP), a joint initiative between NIST and the National Security Agency, is seeking to establish cost-effective testing, evaluation, and certification programs for

---

[17] U.S. Congress. House. Committee on Science. Subcommittee on Technology. *The Changing Face of Healthcare in the Electronic Age,* Mar. 10, 2000. Testimony and opening statements are available online at [http://www.house.gov/science/106_hearing.htm].

information technology security products. The program will benefit producers by increasing the value and competitiveness of their products through the availability of formal, independent testing and certificates of validation. NIAP efforts will also help users by providing a sound and reliable basis for the evaluation, comparison, and selection of security products.[18]

Working together with industry, NIAP is using the Common Criteria for Information Technology Security Evaluation to develop generic testing specifications for particular information technology products. The Common Criteria are a set of internationally developed standards for evaluating the security properties of information technology products and systems. Last year, NIAP and NIST helped establish an industry-led health care security forum to discuss security requirements for health care information technology systems, and the potential for developing specific sets of security requirements using the Common Criteria.

PRIVACY RULE: OVERVIEW AND ISSUES

On December 28, 2000, HHS published a final rule to protect the privacy of medical records and other personally identifiable health information.[19] The rule took effect on April 14, 2001(see **Table 2**).[20] Covered entities have 2 years (i.e., April 14, 2003) to come into compliance.[21] The privacy rule covers health care providers who electronically transmit health information in connection with one of the HIPAA specified transactions, health plans, and health care clearinghouses. HIPAA did not provide HHS with the authority to regulate directly the actions of other entities that collect and maintain health information, such as life insurers, researchers, and employers (unless they are acting as providers or plans). However, the rule requires covered entities to enter into contracts with each of their business associates with whom they share personal health information for purposes

---

[18] NIAP information is available online at [http://niap.nist.gov].
[19] 65 *Federal Register* 82461–82829. 20
[20] Initially, the privacy rule was set to take effect on February 26, 2001. However, that date was delayed in accordance with the Congressional Review Act of 1996, which requires a major rule to be submitted to Congress for a 60-day review period before it becomes effective. Congress did not receive the rule from HHS until February 13, thereby pushing back the effective date to April 14.
[21] Small health plans with annual receipts of no more than $5 million have an additional year (i.e., April 14, 2004) to comply.

other than consultation, referral, or treatment.[22] The contracts bind the business associates to comply with the covered entities' privacy practices and safeguard the confidentiality of protected health information.

Table 3 summarizes the key provisions of the health privacy rule, which applies to all personally identifiable health information handled by covered entities, regardless of the form or format in which it is maintained or transmitted.[23] The rule establishes new rights for patients regarding access to and use of their health information. It gives patients the right to view and copy their medical records, request that their medical records be amended, and obtain a history of authorized disclosures of their records. Covered entities must provide patients with written notice of their privacy procedures and the anticipated uses and disclosures of patient information. Patients will also be able to file a complaint with HHS if they believe their privacy rights have been violated.

The rule establishes two distinct forms of patient release for the use and disclosure of identifiable health information. First, providers must obtain a patient's one-time, general consent to use or disclose their information for treatment, payment, and other health care operations. Providers may make patient consent a condition of receiving treatment. Health plans and clearinghouses have the option to obtain patient consent to use and disclose health information for their own health care operations. The general consent document must inform patients of their privacy rights, including the right to request restrictions on the use and disclosure of their medical information for routine health care functions.

Second, all covered entities must obtain a patient's specific authorization in order to use or disclose information for non-routine uses and most non-health care purposes, such as releasing information to lending institutions or life insurers. The authorization form must specify the type of information to be disclosed, the person(s) authorized to disclose the information, and the person(s) who will receive the information.

The rule specifies certain national priority activities in which patient information may be used and disclosed without authorization, consistent with other applicable laws and regulations. These activities include health care system oversight, public health activities, research (see discussion below), and law enforcement. Covered entities may also use certain patient

---

[22] A business associate is any person or organization that performs a function involving the use or disclosure of identifiable health information on behalf of a covered entity or provides legal, actuarial, accounting, or other services.

[23] Medical information in education records covered by the Family Educational Right and Privacy Act (FERPA) is excluded from the privacy rule.

information, without first seeking authorization, to develop mailing lists for fundraising appeals, but they must give patients the opportunity to opt out of receiving future appeals. Also, while the rule prohibits covered entities from releasing patient information to marketing companies without prior authorization, a covered entity may itself use such information for marketing on behalf of third parties, provided patients are given the opportunity to opt out of receiving further marketing communications.

With the exception of uses and disclosures of patient information for the purpose of treatment, covered entities must limit the information disclosed to the minimum necessary to accomplish the purpose of disclosure. Within covered entities, employees' access to health information must be limited to the minimum needed to do their jobs. Employers that sponsor health plans may not obtain and use employees' health information for purposes unrelated to providing and paying for health care (e.g., hiring and promotion decisions) without explicit authorization.

Concerns and Issues Dividing Stakeholders

A coalition of hospitals, health maintenance organizations, insurers, and pharmaceutical companies mounted an aggressive lobbying effort at the beginning of the year to scale back the privacy rule. These groups are critical of the rule's general consent requirement, the minimum necessary standard, and business associate contracts. They claim that the rule, as currently written, will compromise patient care by placing unacceptable restrictions on access to health information and be extremely costly to implement. The critics had hoped to delay the rule's implementation and reopen the rulemaking process to amend the rule and make it administratively and financially less burdensome.

On February 28, the Bush Administration responded to the health care industry's concerns by opening the rule for an additional 30-day period of public comment.[24] After the comment period closed on March 30, HHS officials indicated that they would likely delay implementation of the rule in order to make changes to simplify it and lessen its financial burden. However, the Administration announced on April 12 that the rule would take effect on schedule.

Patient privacy advocates firmly support the health privacy rule, though they too have concerns with some of its provisions. They are chiefly

---

[24] 66 *Federal Register* 12738–12739.

concerned about the constraints that HIPAA placed on HHS. They favor legislation that would allow the agency to broaden federal privacy protections to cover all entities that handle medical information and provide patients with the right to sue in federal court for violations of their health information privacy. Consumer advocacy groups have fought health care industry efforts to lobby HHS for modifications to the rule, which they claim would weaken the rule's privacy protections.

Stakeholders presented their views on the privacy rule in testimony before the Senate Health, Education, Labor, and Pensions Committee and the House Energy and Commerce Subcommittee on Health in early 2001.[25] Key concerns and issues raised during those hearings, which are likely to remain central to the debate over the rule's implementation, are discussed below.

Patient Consent

The most controversial provision in the privacy rule is the requirement that health care providers obtain patient consent prior to using or disclosing health information for treatment, payment, and other health care operations. Consent is optional for providers who have an indirect relationship with patients (i.e., they have no direct contact with the patient, or they provide services at the request of another provider). Health plans and clearinghouses also have the option, but are not required, to obtain consent in order to use or disclose information for payment and health care operations. Patients have the right to request restrictions on how their information is used or disclosed, though covered entities are not required to agree to any such restrictions. Patients may revoke their consent at any time.

Privacy advocates and the American Medical Association (AMA) support the requirement that direct health care providers must obtain consent prior to routine uses and disclosures, but question why health plans and clearinghouses are not held to the same standard. According to the AMA, patient trust in the health care system can only be assured when all entities that maintain health information have an obligation to safeguard the confidentiality of that information, and when patients have control over decisions by those entities to use and disclose the information. Requiring consent before any use or disclosure of health information for health care operations also creates an incentive to de-identify information at the earliest possible opportunity.

---

[25] The Senate HELP Committee hearing was held on February 8, and the House Health Subcommittee hearing was held on March 22. Testimony is available on the committee Web sites [http://www.senate.gov/~labor]; [http://www.house.gov/commerce].

The AMA is especially concerned that consent is optional for health plans in view of the rule's broad definition of health care operations. The definition includes conducting quality assessment and improvement activities; reviewing and evaluating provider performance, and health plan performance; underwriting, premium rating, and other activities relating to the creation, renewal or replacement of health insurance contract; conducting or arranging for medical review, legal services, and auditing functions; and business planning, development, and management. The AMA contends that the definition of health care operations is sufficiently broad to encompass virtually all uses of information.

Health insurers are extremely critical of the consent requirement. They point out that physicians will be unable to use patient information without a signed consent, and that the effort and cost of obtaining consent from over 200 million Americans will be daunting. They also fear that the consent requirement may unintentionally delay and impede routine operations that are essential to providing quality care and timely payment. For example, when a physician calls in a prescription, the pharmacist would need to have the patient's consent on file in order to fill the prescription and process the insurance claim. Family members and friends would also be unable to pick up prescriptions on behalf of the patient.

Privacy advocates dismiss these arguments as misplaced and inaccurate. They point out that the rule permits covered entities to use their professional judgement and experience in allowing family members and others to pick up items like prescriptions, medical supplies, or x-rays. They also believe that the problem of a pharmacist needing a patient's consent on file in advance of filling a prescription is easily remedied. HHS could, for example, issue a guidance that would allow a pharmacist in such a situation to be considered to have an indirect treatment relationship with the patient.

The American Hospital Association (AHA) has complained that it did not have adequate opportunity to comment on how the prior consent provision would impact patient care or hospital operations. HHS did not include prior consent in the proposed rule, though the agency did invite comments on whether other approaches to protecting health information would be more effective. The agency added the consent provision to the final rule in response to the comments it received. The AHA is also concerned about the impact of the consent requirement on routine hospital operations. For example, hospitals would be unable to obtain background medical information and schedule surgery without first getting a patient's consent.

Minimum Necessary

Stakeholders are also divided over the requirement that, with the exception of treatment-related disclosures, covered entities must make a reasonable effort to disclose no more than the minimum amount of information necessary to accomplish the intended purpose of the disclosure. The minimum necessary standard also applies to internal uses of information and requires entities to define what information will be made available to each employee by role.

Privacy advocates and the AMA are generally supportive of the minimum necessary standard. Physicians are responsible for determining the minimum amount necessary, except when responding to requests for information from health insurers, in which case it becomes the responsibility of the payer to request only the minimum amount necessary. The AMA is concerned that some health plans may request more information than a physician would judge to be the minimum necessary. However, the rule allows physicians to review all non-routine requests to determine whether they meet the minimum necessary standard. The AMA supports the exception to the minimum necessary standard for disclosures to or requests by a health care provider for treatment purposes, which is designed to give physicians the freedom to exchange and review information to provide patients the treatment they need.

The AMA is critical of the requirement that physician's offices establish and implement policies and procedures for complying with the minimum necessary standard, and review non-routine requests for disclosures. It questions the added benefit of such a requirement in view of physicians' ethical and professional obligations to keep patient information confidential.

Health insurers argue that the minimum necessary standard could jeopardize the quality of patient care. Most health care services today are delivered in an integrated system. Health plans are concerned that the minimum necessary standard will limit the flow of information that they say is essential to good patient care and prompt payment. HMOs, in particular, fear that physicians might use the minimum necessary standard to justify withholding patient information. Insurers are also critical of the fact that the exemption for treatment purposes covers only disclosures of information and not uses of information. As a result, the rule may limit a physician's access to vital information during critical treatment situations. In fact, the rule allows the use of the entire medical record when it is specifically justified as the amount that is reasonably necessary to accomplish the purpose of the use.[26]

Business Associate Contracts

The rule requires covered entities to enter into contracts with their business associates to ensure that these groups, which are not directly covered by HIPAA, adhere to the same privacy protections.[27] HHS adopted this arrangement as a way of extending the rule's protections to information shared with others in the health care system. The agency proposed requiring covered entities to monitor the activities of their business associates. That language was amended in the final rule by limiting a covered entity's liability to those circumstances where the entity has knowledge of a breach of contract by the business associate and fails to take action. The rule exempts providers from having to enter into contracts when the disclosure of patient information is for treatment purposes. Examples of such exemptions include consultations between physicians at separate facilities, and physicians writing prescriptions to be filled by pharmacists.

Patients rights groups have applauded the use of business associate contracts, though they point out that many entities that handle health information remain unregulated (e.g., financial institutions, marketing firms, researchers, and employers who are not acting as providers or plans). They view the rule as an intermediate step and have urged Congress to pass a more comprehensive health privacy law applicable to all entities that handle personal health information.

Health plans, employers, and provider groups are opposed to the business associate contracts, which they argue will result in covered entities having to develop hundreds, if not thousands, of privacy contracts. They complain that drafting the contracts will be a lengthy and complex process. Privacy advocates respond that the rule's implementation specifications for business associate contracts are clear and straightforward and should not result in complicated contracts. In order to reduce the administrative burden, covered entities have the option of developing standard contracts or standard addenda to existing contracts.

---

[26] HHS states, in the preamble to the rule, that it expects that covered entities will implement policies that allow persons involved in treatment to have access to the entire record, as needed.

[27] The rule defines business associates based on their relationship with covered entities. A business associate is any individual or entity, other than a member of the workforce of a covered entity, which provides services to or on behalf of a covered entity and uses or discloses personal health information that belongs to a covered entity. Business associates include accountants, attorneys, auditors, and billing and data management firms.

The rule requires business associates to use and disclose health information in accordance with the policies and procedures established by the covered entity with whom they contract. Critics are concerned that business associates who contract with multiple covered entities may find themselves subject to differing standards. The situation is further complicated by the fact that some covered entities, such as health insurers, may also act as business associates to other covered entities. Health plans argue that keeping track of all these potential relationships and contractual obligations will be confusing and time-consuming.

Accrediting bodies, such as the Joint Commission for the Accreditation of Healthcare Organizations (JCAHO), claim that they act as health oversight agencies on behalf of government programs and should not be treated as business associates. JCAHO estimates that it would need to enter into contracts with each of the 18,000 facilities—including hospitals, nursing homes, and home health agencies—that it surveys for accreditation. Several groups contend that HHS exceeded its statutory authority by including the business associate contract provisions in the rule. They point out that HIPAA clearly delineates the entities that are covered under the rule (i.e., health plans, clearinghouses, and providers conducting standard electronic transactions).

Marketing by Covered Entities

Patient advocacy groups are concerned about a provision in the rule that allows physicians, hospitals, and other covered entities (or their business associates) to market products and services to patients without their prior authorization. For example, health care providers are permitted to use or disclose a patient's medical information to prescribe, recommend or sell their own products and services, or the products and services of others, as part of the treatment of that individual. Covered entities must identify themselves when making a marketing appeal, indicate whether they are being paid to do so, and give patients the opportunity to opt out of receiving any further such communications.

Commercial use of patient information without authorization is one of the issues that is fueling the public's health privacy concerns. Representatives of patient advocacy groups caution that public confidence in the privacy rule may suffer as a result of the marketing provision. They would like the rule amended to give patients the opportunity to opt out in advance of all marketing communications. Such a change in the rule, they argue, would help allay the public's concerns.

Research

The Association of American Medical Colleges (AAMC), which represents the nation's medical schools and teaching hospitals, has raised several concerns about the potentially negative impact of the rule on medical research. Epidemiologists and health services researchers rely on access to archived, de-identified patient records in order to study the incidence and expression of diseases in specified populations, the beneficial and adverse outcomes of new therapies, and the cost-effectiveness of the health care system. However, the AAMC fears that in order the meet the rule's definition of de-identified information, medical records have to be stripped of so many identifying elements as to render them useless for most research. The association favors a de-identification standard that reflects the realities of medical research and the motivations of researchers, rather than one which it claims is designed to address the exaggerated fear of threats from decryption experts with criminal intentions.

The AAMC is also critical of some of the rule's new criteria that must be met in order for researchers to obtain a waiver of patient authorization to access identifiable health information. Federally funded research involving human subjects, and clinical trials of new drugs and medical devices, are subject to a set of federal regulations called the Common Rule. Under the Common Rule, research proposals must be approved by an Institutional Review Board (IRB) to ensure that the rights and welfare of the research subjects are protected. IRBs also decide whether or not to waive informed consent based on the level of risk to the participants. The health privacy rule requires all research involving human subjects, regardless of its source of funding, to undergo review by an IRB or a newly created Privacy Board (PB). The IRB or PB must determine that the research meets eight new criteria regarding privacy rights and risks, in addition to the provisions of the Common Rule, before it can approve a waiver. The AAMC is concerned that some of the criteria are contradictory and that IRBs have no experience or training to make those determinations.

For research performed under an informed consent waiver, the rule requires the IRB or PB to determine that the information requested by the investigator meets the minimum necessary requirement. The AAMC is unclear how IRB or PB members will be able to make this determination in judging proposals for research that requires access to very large medical databases. Moreover, the association is concerned that the expectation that the minimum necessary standard has been met will generate a risk of liability for covered entities. Add to that the rule's general complexity and the administrative burdens it places of covered entities, and the AAMC argues that covered entities may be reluctant to make health information accessible to researchers.

State Law Preemption

Preemption of state laws is one of the most controversial issues in the health privacy debate. As required by HIPAA, the rule does not preempt state laws that are more protective of individual privacy. Although most states do not have comprehensive health privacy laws, nearly all states have condition-specific privacy requirements that protect individuals with mental illness, communicable diseases (e.g., HIV/AIDS), cancer, and other sensitive or stigmatized diseases from having their health information disclosed without their authorization. Such laws aim to bolster public trust and confidence in the health care system and encourage patients to seek treatment and counseling without fear of disclosure of sensitive information. Under the rule, those condition-specific protections would remain in effect. However, less protective state laws would be preempted. The rule, therefore, serves as a baseline (i.e., a federal "floor") of minimum privacy protection.

The rule allows any person to submit to the Secretary in writing a request to exempt a provision of state law from preemption. It is unclear from the rule to what extent, and how, the Secretary will allow public comment on such preemption decisions.

Large health plans and employers that operate in more than one state have strongly criticized the rule for not preempting all state laws to create a single, national privacy standard for health information. They argue that the rule's partial preemption of state law will be extremely burdensome and costly to implement and only add to the difficulties of navigating through the existing maze of state privacy laws. Critics of the rule's preemption provisions contend that covered entities will have to maintain some form of state-to-federal regulation matrix to ensure that they are complying with the correct laws and/or regulations. Because HIPAA specifically provided for establishing a federal floor of privacy protections, several stakeholders are calling for new legislation to establish full federal preemption.

Patient and privacy advocates, state governments, and providers strongly support partial federal preemption, as provided in the rule. They believe that a federal floor guarantees a minimum level of protection for everyone, while still allowing states to enact more stringent protections and address future privacy concerns. A recent survey of state health privacy statutes suggests that the rule would significantly improve the privacy protections afforded to patients' medical information by requiring states with fairly minimal privacy protections to come up to the federal baseline.[28]

Privacy advocates are critical of a provision that excludes state parental notification laws from the rule's general preemption requirements. Under the rule, laws that authorize (or prohibit) disclosure of health information about a minor to a parent or guardian would not be preempted. Advocates for patients' privacy argue that minors should enjoy the same protections as adults. However, some conservative groups are opposed to minors being able to conceal reproductive health information from their parents (e.g., use of birth control, abortion).

Finally, HIPAA excludes state public health laws from federal preemption. States have traditionally exercised oversight and authority over public health. Under the rule, therefore, disclosures made for public health purposes, as mandated by state laws, do not require patient authorization. Such laws include reporting diseases and injuries, collecting vital statistics, public health surveillance, and public health investigation and intervention.

Compliance Costs

Groups that represent health plans and health care providers have criticized HHS' impact analysis and expressed concern about the potential cost of complying with the privacy rule. HHS estimates that the rule will cost $17.6 billion over 10 years. Two provisions—restricting disclosures to the minimum amount of necessary information and establishing a privacy official—account from more than half of HHS' cost estimate. According to the agency, the cost of the privacy rule is more than offset by implementation of the transaction and code sets rule, which is estimated to save the health care industry $29.9 over 10 years. Together, the two rules will produce a net savings of about $12.3 billion in improved health care efficiency and privacy protection.

Industry groups believe that the actual compliance costs will substantially exceed HHS' estimates. An independent assessment commissioned by the Blue Cross Blue Shield Association (BCBSA) estimated that the proposed health privacy rule would cost the health care industry more than $40 billion over 5 years. According to the BCBSA, most of these costs remain applicable to the final rule. The BCBSA also believes that HHS overestimated the savings from implementing the transactions standards.

---

[28] *The State of Health Privacy: An Uneven Terrain* was prepared in 1999 by the Health Privacy Project and is available online at [http://www.healthprivacy.org].

A study commissioned by the AHA, looking at hospital costs alone, found that the cost of only three key provisions of the proposed rule—minimum necessary, business associates, and state law preemption—could be as much as $22.5 billion over 5 years. Other provider groups are concerned that spending additional time with patients to explain the rule's requirements and obtain consent will compete with time for direct patient care.

Several groups have expressed concern about being able to implement the rule within the two-year time frame. Despite their concerns, however, organizations that represent plans and providers are developing model forms for patient consent, notices explaining privacy practices, business associate contracts, and compliance plans.

HHS Implementation Guidelines

HHS sources have indicated that the agency is about to release a detailed guidance document to help covered entities implement the privacy rule. The document is expected to address industry concerns by providing explanations of intent and clarifying some of the rule's key provisions. It is unclear to what extent, if any, the implementation guidelines will alter the rule. Under HIPAA, the Secretary has the authority to modify the rule after it takes effect in order to permit compliance. However, any significant modifications to the rule's provisions would require reopening the rulemaking process.

LEGISLATIVE ACTIVITY IN THE 107TH CONGRESS

Lawmakers have introduced two bills (S. 836, H.R. 1975) that would delay the scheduled compliance dates of HIPAA's Administrative Simplification standards (i.e., transactions and codes, security, and unique identifiers). Both bills would set October 16, 2004 as the uniform compliance date, or 24 months after all the final rules are published, whichever is later. Neither bill directly covers the privacy rule, and H.R. 1975 includes language that specifically excludes the privacy rule from its provisions.

The legislation is in response to efforts by Blue Cross Blue Shield (BCBS) and other health care industry groups to delay implementation of HIPAA until all the standards and enforcement regulations, with the exception of the privacy rule, are published in final form. BCBS claims that without this extension there will be substantial disruptions in payments to providers. In congressional testimony, industry groups stressed the importance of synchronizing the compliance dates for the HIPAA standards to ensure that covered entities have a complete picture of what is required before they purchase new information technology systems and retrain their employees. They argue that having to comply with each new rule in turn will only add to HIPAA's overall administrative and financial burden.

ADDITIONAL INFORMATION AND WEB SITES

Detailed information on all the HIPAA standards, including the text of all *Federal Register* notices, summaries of all proposed and final regulations, public comments, and the HHS implementation plant can be found on the department's Administrative Simplification home page [http://aspe.hhs.gov/admnsimp]. HHS's Office of Civil Rights, which is responsible for implementing and enforcing the privacy rule and is responding to questions about the rule. Additional information on the HIPAA Administrative Simplification standards may be found at the following Web sites.

General HIPAA Information

Phoenix Health Systems [http://www.hipaadvisory.com]
HIPAA Comply [http://www.hipaacomply.com]
National Committee on Vital and Health Statistics [http://ncvhs.hhs.gov]

Electronic Transactions and Code Sets

Accredited Standards Committee X12 [http://www.x12.org]
Washington Pub. Co. (X12N implementation guides) [http://www.wpc-edi.com]
National Uniform Billing Committee [http://www.nubc.org]
National Uniform Claims Committee [http://www.nucc.org]
National Council for Prescription Drug Programs [http://www.ncpdp.org]
Workgroup for Electronic Data Interchange [http://www.wedi.org]
Medicaid HIPAA Information [http://www.hcfa.gov/medicaid/hipaa/adminsim]
HCPCS [http://www.hcfa.gov/medicare/hcpcs.htm]

Privacy

Patient Privacy Advocates
Health Privacy Project, Washington DC [http://www.healthprivacy.org]
National Coalition for Patient Rights [http://www.nationalcpr.org]
American Civil Liberties Union [http://www.aclu.org]

Health Care Plans, Providers, and Clearinghouses
Association for Electronic Health Care Transactions [http://www.afehct.org]
American Health Information Management Association [http://www.ahima.org]
American Hospital Association [http://www.aha.org]
American Medical Association [http://www.ama-assn.org]
American Association of Health Plans [http://www.aahp.org]
Health Insurance Association of America [http://www.hiaa.org]
Blue Cross Blue Shield Association [http://www.bluecares.com]
Association of American Medical Colleges [http://www.aamc.org]

GAO Reports

GAO has provided the Senate Committee on Health Education, Labor, and Pensions with analysis of the health privacy rule. The following reports are available on GAO's Web site [http://www.gao.gov].

Privacy Standards: Issues in HHS' Proposed Rule on Confidentiality of Personal Health Information, GAO/T-HEHS-00-106, April 6, 2000.

Health Privacy: Regulation Enhances Protection of Patient Records but Raises Practical Concerns, GAO/T-01-387, Feb. 8, 2001.

Medical Privacy Regulation: Questions Remain About Implementing the New Consent Requirement, GAO-01-584, April 6, 2001.

Table 1. Summary of HIPAA's Administrative Simplification Provisions

Purpose (Section 261)	To improve the efficiency and effectiveness of the health care system by establishing standards and requirements for the electronic transmission of certain types of health information. Amends Title XI of the Social Security Act by adding Part C—Administrative Simplification.
Administrative Simplification (Section 262)	
• Definitions	Defines health care clearinghouse, health care provider, health plan, personally identifiable health information, and standard setting organization.
• General Requirements for Adoption of Standards	Specifies that the standards apply to health plans, health care clearinghouses, and health care providers that transmit health information electronically. Requires the Secretary either to adopt standards that have already been developed by standard setting organizations or to develop different standards, provided they substantially reduce administrative costs to health plans and providers. If no standard has been adopted by a standard setting organization, the Secretary must develop a new standard based on the recommendations of the NCVHS and consultations with standard setting organizations and other appropriate agencies. For all the standards, the Secretary is required to consult with the National Uniform Billing Committee, the National Uniform Claim Committee, the Workgroup for Electronic Data Interchange, and the American Dental Association.
• Standards for Electronic Health Care Transactions	Instructs the Secretary to issue the following standards: (1) Uniform formats for use in the electronic exchange of health information, including health claims and attachments, health plan eligibility and enrollment, and health care payment, and health claim status. (2) Code sets for data elements in standard electronic transactions. (3) Unique identifiers for individuals, employers, health plans, and health care providers. (4) Security standards to provide administrative, technical, and physical safeguards for protecting medical record confidentiality. (5) An electronic signature standard to verify the authenticity of the signer and the transaction.
• Timetable for Adoption of Standards	Requires the Secretary to adopt all the standards within 18 months of HIPAA's enactment (i.e., by February 21, 1998), except for the standards for claims attachments, which are due within 30 months of enactment (i.e., by February 21, 1999). Permits the Secretary to modify the standards as frequently as once every 12 months.
• Requirements for Compliance	Requires health plans and providers that process electronic transactions to use standard formats and data elements. Plans and providers may transmit and receive such data either directly or by contracting with a clearinghouse to convert nonstandard data elements into standard transactions. Gives entities covered by the standards up to 24 months to comply. Small health plans have 36 months to comply. [a]

• **Civil Penalties for Failure to Comply**	Establishes a civil monetary penalty of $100 per person per violation of a specific standard, up to a maximum of $25,000 per person for all such violations in any calender year. Allows the penalty to be waived if the person liable for the penalty did not know, and by exercising reasonable diligence would not have known, that the standard had been violated. Also waives the penalty if failure to comply was due to reasonable cause and not willful neglect.
• **Criminal Penalties for Wrongful Disclosures**	Establishes criminal penalties for wrongfully using a unique health identifier, or wrongfully obtaining or disclosing personally identifiable health information. Penalties range from a $50,000 fine and/or 1 year in prison, up to a $250,000 fine and 10 years in prison if the offense is committed with intent to sell, transfer, or use the information for commercial advantage, personal gain, or do malicious harm.
• **Impact on State Law**	Standards preempt contrary provisions in state law pertaining to health information, including provisions that require medical records to be maintained in written rather than electronic form. However, the standards may not preempt or limit state laws that are necessary to prevent fraud and abuse, regulate health insurance companies, or report on health care delivery and costs. The standards may not limit the authority of states to collect and report public health statistics (e.g., births, deaths, diseases, injuries).
• **Financial Institutions**	Standards do not apply to the processing of payment transactions by financial institutions (e.g., exchanging information during a credit card payment for health care).
• **National Committee on Vital and Health Statistics (Section 263)**	Amends Section 306(k) of the Public Health Service Act to increase NCVHS membership from 16 to 18 members and requires NCVHS to advise the Secretary on issues related to the collection, processing, and tabulation of health statistics. Requires NCVHS to study the adoption of uniform health data standards and the electronic exchange of such information, and report its recommendations to Congress within 4 years of HIPAA's enactment (i.e., by August 21, 2000). Instructs NCVHS to report annually to Congress on the implementation of HIPAA's Administrative Simplification provisions.[b]
• **Health Information Privacy (Section 264)**	Requires the Secretary to submit to Congress within 1 year of HIPAA's enactment (i.e., by August 21, 1997) recommendations for standards to protect the privacy of personally identifiable health information.[c] Mandates the Congress to pass health privacy legislation within 3 years of HIPAA's enactment (i.e., by August 21, 1999), otherwise the Secretary is instructed, in consultation with NCVHS, to issue privacy standards within the following 6 months (i.e., by February 21, 2000). Such standards may not preempt state laws that are more protective of health information privacy.

Source: Text of HIPAA, as enacted into law (P.L. 104-191).

a HCFA defines small health plans as those with annual receipts of $5 million or less.

b NCVHS reports are available on its Web site at [http://www.ncvhs.hhs.gov].

c The Secretary's recommendations, which were presented before the Senate Committee on Labor and Human Resources on September 11, 1997, are available online at [http://aspe.os.dhhs.gov/admnsimp/pvcrec.htm].

Table 2. Implementation Status of HIPAA's Standards

Standards[a]	NPRM[b]	Final Rule	Effective Date[c]
Electronic Transactions and Code Sets	May 7, 1998	August 17, 2000	October 16, 2000
Provider Identifier	May 7, 1998	Expected 2001	
Health Plan Identifier	Expected 2001		
Employer Identifier	June 16, 1998	Expected 2001	
Individual Identifier	*On Hold*		
Security and Electronic Signatures	August 12, 1998	Expected 2001	
Privacy	November 3, 1999	December 28, 2000	April 14, 2001

Source: Health Care Financing Administration.
a HHS plans to issue an enforcement rule that applies to all the HIPAA Administrative Simplification standards. The rule will address the imposition of civil monetary penalties and the referral of criminal cases where there has been a violation of the standards.
b Notice of Proposed Rulemaking.
c Covered entities have 2 years to come into compliance. Small health plans with revenues of $5 million or less have an additional year to comply.

Table 3. Key Provisions of the Health Privacy Rule (45 CFR 160, 164)

Covered Entities	Applies to health care providers who electronically transmit health information in connection with any of the HIPAA-covered transactions, health plans, and health care clearinghouses. [160.102, 164.500]
Covered Health Information	Applies to personally identifiable health information created or received by a covered entity and transmitted or maintained in any form or medium (e.g., paper, electronic, oral). [164.501]
Patient Access	Gives patients the right to access, inspect and copy their health information within 30 days of making a request for access, if the information is maintained or accessible on-site (otherwise within 60 days). Allows covered entities to impose reasonable costbased fees for copying the information. Covered entities may deny access under certain circumstances. [164.524]
Amendment of Health Information	Gives patients the right to request amendment of their health information and requires covered entities to act on such a request within 60 days. Allows covered entities to deny a request if they determine that the patient's information is accurate and complete, or was not created by the covered entity. Permits requester to submit a written statement of disagreement with the denial. [164.526]

Accounting of Disclosures	Gives patients the right to receive, within 60 days, an accounting of disclosures over the past 6 years, except for disclosures for treatment, payment, and health care operations, and for certain other specified purposes. Accounting must include a brief statement of the purpose of each disclosure and the address of the recipient of the information. [164.528]
Patient Notice	Requires covered entities to provide patients with written notice of their privacy rights, as well as notice of the entities' legal duties and privacy practices. Specifies the content of the notice. [164.520]
Minimum Necessary	Requires covered entities to make a reasonable effort to use or disclose the minimum amount of information necessary to accomplish the intended purpose, except for disclosures related to treatment. [164.502(b), 164.514(d)]
De-identified Information	Defines de-identified health information as information from which 18 specified types of identifiers have been removed, or information for which an expert determines that the risk of identification is very small. De-identified information is not subject to the rule. Disclosure of a code or other means of enabling de-identified information to be re-identified constitutes disclosure of protected health information. [164.502(d), 164.514(a)-(c)]
Payment, Treatment, and Health Care Operations	Health care providers must obtain a patient's one-time consent in writing before using or disclosing health information for treatment, payment, or other routine health care operations. Providers may condition treatment on obtaining such consent. (Health plans and clearinghouses may also obtain consent for their own use and disclosure of health information for treatment, payment, or other routine health care operations, and may condition enrollment on obtaining such consent.) Patients have the right to request restrictions on these types of use and disclosure, but covered entities are not required to agree to such a request. Patients may in writing revoke their consent at any time. [164.506, 164.522(a)]
Directory Assistance and Next of Kin	Requires covered entities to give patients notice and the opportunity to opt out before information is disclosed to a facility directory or provided to next of kin or other persons involved in the patients' care. [164.510]
Non-Routine and Non-Health Care Disclosures	Covered entities must obtain a patient's specific authorization in writing before using or disclosing health information for nonroutine uses and most non-health care purposes (see Disclosures Not Requiring Authorization below). Covered entities may not condition services or payment on receipt of such authorization. Patients may revoke their authorization at any time. [164.508]
Business Associates	Allows a covered entity to disclose health information to a business associate without further authorization if it obtains satisfactory assurances, though a written contract, that the business associate will safeguard the information. The contract must establish the permitted and required uses and disclosures of such information by the business associate. A business associate may use health information for its own management and administration, and may disclose it to others if it obtains assurances that the information will be held in confidence and the recipient will notify the business associate of breaches of confidentiality. [164.502(e), 164.504(e)]
Employers	Employers that sponsor health plans may not obtain and use employees' health information for employment or other non-health purposes without their specific authorization. [164.504(f)]

Hybrid Entities	Requires hybrid entities (i.e., companies with multiple lines of business) to restrict disclosure of health information between their health care and non-health care components. Such disclosures are governed by the same restrictions as disclosures between two separate and distinct legal entities. [164.504(b)(c)]
Disclosures Not Requiring Authorization	Covered entities may use and disclose health information without a patient's authorization for the following national priority activities, consistent with other applicable laws and regulations: (a) uses and disclosures required by law; (b) public health activities; (c) abuse, neglect, and domestic violence; (d) health oversight; (e) judicial and administrative proceedings; (f) law enforcement; (g) coroners, medical examiners, and funeral directors; (h) organ donation and transplantation; (i) research; (j) imminent and serious threats to health and safety; (k) specialized government functions; (l) workers' compensation programs. [164.512]
Marketing and Fundraising	Covered entities may use or disclose information without a patient's authorization to market their own products and services, or the products and services of others, as part of the treatment of that individual. Covered entities must identify themselves when making a marketing appeal and give patients the opportunity to opt out of any further communications. Covered entities also may disclose certain patient information to a foundation or business associate that contacts patients for fundraising purposes, provided that patients are given the opportunity to opt out of any further communications. [164.514(e)(f)]
Psychotherapy Notes	Provides higher level of protection than for other types of health information. Requires authorization for most uses or disclosures. Health plans may not condition enrollment or eligibility for benefits on obtaining such authorization. [164.508(a)(2)]
Preemption of State Laws	Preempts all contrary state laws unless they are more stringent (i.e., more protective of privacy). Does not preempt state parental notification laws or state laws used to administer health care, regulate controlled substances, or protect public health, safety and welfare. Allows states to apply to HHS for a determination on whether a state law meets the requirements of these exclusions. [160.201 et seq.]
Safeguards	Requires covered entities to establish and implement various administrative procedures, commensurate with the size and scope of their business, to protect the confidentiality of health information. These include designating a privacy officer, training employees, and developing a system of sanctions for employees who violate an entity's privacy policies. [164.530]
Compliance	Permits an individual, who believes a covered entity is not compliant, to file a written complaint with the Secretary. Authorizes Secretary to conduct a compliance review of such an entity. [160.300 et seq.]
Enforcement	HIPAA imposes civil monetary penalties against covered entities that fail to comply with the rule and imposes criminal penalties for certain wrongful disclosures of health information. Civil fines are $100 per person for unintentional disclosures, capped at $25,000 per year. Criminal penalties for selling, transferring, or using health information for commercial advantage, personal gain, or malicious harm include fines of up to $250,000 and/or up to 10 years in prison. [42 USC 1320d-5,6]

Chapter 4

A BRIEF SUMMARY OF THE HIPAA MEDICAL PRIVACY RULE[*]

Gina Marie Stevens

INTRODUCTION

This chapter provides a brief overview of the modified HIPAA Privacy rule, "Standards for the Privacy of Individually Identifiable Health Information"("privacy rule") published on August 14, 2002 by the Department of Health and Human Services (HHS).[1] Issuance of the modified Privacy Rule by the Bush Administration is the culmination of a decades long debate over access to medical records that has pitted privacy advocates and civil libertarians against employers and much of the health care industry. As required by the Health Insurance Portability and Accountability Act of 1996 ("HIPAA"), a privacy rule was issued in December 2000, and modified August 2002. The privacy rule went into effect April 14, 2001, with compliance required by April 2003 for most entities.[2] The HIPAA Privacy Rule establishes a set of basic consumer protections and a series of regulatory permissions for uses and disclosures of protected health

---

[*] Excerpted from CRS Report RS20934. April 30, 2003.
[1] [http://www.hhs.gov/ocr/combinedregtext.pdf].
[2] See CRS Report RS21505, *Compliance with the HIPAA Medical Privacy Rule*, by Gina Stevens.

information. S. 16, introduced in the 108th Congress by Senator Daschle, would reverse some modifications to the rule. This report will be updated.

BACKGROUND

In recent years, our society has come to rely increasingly on medical information to perform basic functions and to make decisions about individuals. However, a number of fundamental developments have threatened the confidentiality of health-care information, and are the cause of a great deal of concern. The emergence of third-party payment plans; the use of health-care information for non-health care purposes; the growing involvement of government agencies in virtually all aspects of health care; and the exponential increase in the use of computers and automated information systems for health record information have combined to put substantial pressure on traditional confidentiality protections. In addition, an increasing number of parties involved in health care treatment, payment, and oversight have routine access to personally identifiable health records. Greater utilization of health-care information coupled with inadequate confidentiality protections has increased the potential for unauthorized uses and disclosures of medical information. The disclosure of personally identifiable health-care information can profoundly affect people's lives. "It affects decisions on whether they are hired or fired; whether they can secure business licenses, and life insurance; whether they are permitted to drive cars; whether they are placed under police surveillance or labeled a security risk; or even whether they can get nominated for and elected to political office."[3] Other secondary uses of health-care information, such as the use of genetic test results for employment and insurance purposes, have the potential to result in harm to the health-care subject if the information is disclosed for unauthorized purposes. These factors accentuate the need for strong legal safeguards.

Medical Privacy Laws

The confidentiality of health-care information is governed by various federal, state, and local statutes, ordinances, regulations, and case law. Also applicable are private accreditation standards, such as those of the Joint

---

[3] A. Westin, *Computers, Health Records, and Citizen's Rights* 60 (1976).

Commission on Accreditation of Healthcare Organizations, internal policies of particular institutions, and ethical guidelines of professional organizations. Prior to the issuance of the HIPAA privacy rule, federal laws did not address the confidentiality of health-care information collected and maintained by the private sector (*i.e.*, doctors, hospitals, health plans, health insurers, and other health-care related entities). A major impetus for the enactment of HIPAA's privacy requirement was the absence of a comprehensive federal law that protected the confidentiality of patient records in all settings.

Another impetus for the enactment of HIPAA was the lack of uniformity among the states in their treatment of the confidentiality of health-care information. There was substantial variation between the states on many aspects of medical records law. These differences are becoming much more critical in the collection, maintenance, and disclosure of health-care information as it is transmitted through interstate commerce amongst patients, physicians, health-care facilities, employers, government agencies, and insurers located in different states and subject to different laws. To address this disparity, HIPAA provides that state law, except for certain specified laws (concerning public health surveillance) and state laws that are more stringent, is preempted by the federal privacy rule. A compendium of state laws issued July 20, 1999 and November 2002 by Georgetown University's Health Privacy Project, "The State of Health Privacy: An Uneven Terrain", identifies medical records privacy provisions from state legislative codes. The report covers only state statutes and divides them by patient access, restrictions on disclosure, privilege, and condition specific requirements.[4]

HIPAA

Several comprehensive medical records confidentiality bills were introduced during the past decade, with the end result being passage of the medical privacy requirements as part of the Health Insurance Portability and Accountability Act of 1996 ("HIPAA"). The Health Insurance Portability and Accountability Act of 1996 (HIPAA), Pub. L. 104-191, 42 U.S.C. §§ 1320d *et seq.*, was created to improve the portability and continuity of health insurance coverage, to combat waste, fraud and abuse in health care, to promote the use of medical savings accounts, to improve access to long term care, and to simplify the administration of health insurance. Sections 261

---

[4] See, [http://www.healthprivacy.org/info-url_nocat2304/info-url_nocat.htm].

through 264 of HIPAA are known as the administrative simplification provisions. The general administrative simplification rule requires health care payers and providers who transmit transactions electronically to use standardized data elements to conduct financial and administrative transactions. Section 262 directs HHS to issue standards to facilitate the electronic exchange of information, and to develop standards to protect the security of such information. Section 264 of HIPAA requires HHS to submit to the Congress detailed recommendations on standards with respect to privacy rights for individually identifiable health information.

The Secretary made preliminary privacy recommendations to Congress in September 1997, based on the core fair information principles of notice, consent, access, security, and enforcement/redress, to: limit the use of an individual's health care information to health purposes only; require organizations to provide adequate security measures to protect information from misuse or disclosure; provide patients with new rights to control how their health information is used, such as the ability to get copies of records and propose corrections; hold those who misuse personal health information accountable, and provide redress for persons harmed by its misuse through criminal and civil penalties; and balance privacy protections with public responsibility to support national priorities, including public health, research, quality care, and reduction of fraud and abuse, including allowing law enforcement access to personal health information. In the 106th Congress several proposals to protect health information were considered, but Congress did not pass legislation. None of the bills were reported out of committee, with disagreements over the patient's right to sue, parental notification of minor's access to health care, and preemption precluding agreement. In the absence of the enactment of federal legislation, HIPAA required HHS to issue privacy regulations.

The December 2000 Privacy Rule

The final privacy regulation was published in the *Federal Register* on December 28, 2000 at 65 Fed. Reg. 82462, shortly before the Clinton Administration left office, and after HHS received over 52,000 comments on its initial proposal. Its original effective date of February 26, 2001 was subsequently changed to April 14, 2001.[5] Enforcement of the rule begins in

---

[5] 66 Fed. Reg. 12433 (Feb. 26, 2001)(the delayed effective date occurred as a result of HHS' failure to submit the rule to Congress for the required 60-day review period until February 13, 2001); *see also* 5 U.S.C. § 801(a)(1).

April 2003, except for small health plans (annual receipts of $5 million or less) who have until 2004 to comply. The medical privacy rule prohibits covered entities from disclosing protected health information to any third parties, unless the rules otherwise permit the disclosure.

Applicability

The rule covers health plans, health care providers, and health care clearinghouses (entities that process or facilitate the processing of nonstandard data elements of health information into standard data elements). It only covers information that is electronically transmitted or maintained. It covers protected health information in any form, whether oral, written or electronic.

Individual Rights

Individuals are given a right of access to their health information, a right to receive notice of the covered entity's privacy policies, a right to request amendments of their information, a right to an accounting of the disclosures made, and a right to file complaints regarding use or disclosure of their information. Individuals may request that restrictions be placed on the disclosure of their health information.

Permitted Uses and Disclosures With Consent or Authorization

The use of protected health information for treatment, payment, or health care operations (a provider's or health plan's management and other activities necessary for support of treatment or payment) requires the prior written consent of a patient. Disclosures for purposes other than treatment, payment, and health care operations require a prior written authorization.

Permitted Uses and Disclosures without Consent or Authorization

Certain public priority uses and disclosures of information do not require prior written consent or authorization (such as health system oversight, public health activities, certain research activities, law enforcement, judicial and administrative proceedings, emergency treatment, and imminent threats to the health or safety of any person). Covered entities are permitted to disclose information to law enforcement for purposes of health care oversight (i.e., investigations of health care fraud, government program fraud, and civil rights investigations), for general law enforcement investigations (i.e., in response to grand jury subpoenas and court orders), to avert a serious threat to health and safety, to coroners and medical examiners, for investigations involving abuse, neglect, or domestic violence.

Information Practice

Disclosures of protected health information other than for treatment purposes must use only the "minimum necessary" information. Covered entities must enter into contracts with "business associates" requiring them to protect individual health information, and must take action if they know of practices by their business associates that violate the contractual agreement. Covered entities must adhere to specific procedures in using information for fundraising or marketing. There are special requirements that apply to both federal and privately funded research. Psychotherapy notes may not be used or disclosed to others without explicit authorization.

Preemption

State law, except for certain specified laws (concerning public health surveillance) and state laws that are more stringent, is preempted by the federal rule.

Enforcement

The Secretary, covered entities, and others are required to ascertain compliance with, and enforcement of the privacy regulation. Any person may file a complaint with the HHS Office for Civil Rights. In cases of noncompliance, the Secretary is directed to resolve the matter by informal means. If the matter cannot be resolved informally, the Secretary may issue written findings of non-compliance that may be used as a basis for initiating action (civil monetary penalties) or a criminal referral.

Penalties

Violators will be subject to civil monetary penalties ($100 per violation up to $25,000 per year), and criminal penalties (up to $250,000 and imprisonment up to 10 years) against covered entities that knowingly and improperly disclose identifiable health information. The regulation does not authorize patients to sue. Instead, the law provides that individuals must direct their complaints to HHS' Office for Civil Rights (OCR).[6] OCR maintains a Web site with information on the new regulation, including guidance at [http://www.hhs.gov/ocr/hipaa/]. HHS also recently issued a 20 page "Summary of the HIPAA Privacy Rule."[7] HHS will enforce the civil

---

[6] See [http://www.ehcca.com/presentations/hipaa6/campanelli.pdf].
[7] [http://www.hhs.gov/ocr/privacysummary.pdf].

money penalties, and the Department of Justice will enforce the criminal penalties.

The final privacy rule was criticized by some for its complexity, and for the imposition of substantial administrative and financial burdens on the health care industry. At the same time, the regulation was applauded by privacy advocates, consumer groups, and some health care industry participants. The General Accounting Office found that considerable uncertainty existed regarding the actions needed to comply with the new privacy regulations. Major concerns among stakeholder groups and the Congress centered on consent and authorization procedures; contractual liability and business associates; parental access to minors' health information (typically related to substance abuse, mental health treatment, and reproductive care); preemption of state laws; law enforcement access to protected health information; costs; and technical assistance.

The August 2002 Privacy Rule

The Bush Administration and HHS re-opened the privacy rule to additional comment on February 8, 2001,[8] and announced that it would accept further comments on the rule until March 30, 2001, see 66 Fed. Reg. 12378. The scope and cost of the rule, coupled with the substantial nature of some concerns raised in the initial comment period, led HHS to conclude that an additional comment period was warranted. On April 12, 2001, Secretary Thompson announced that HHS would immediately begin the process of implementing the patient privacy rule, of issuing guidelines, and of considering any necessary modifications. Several areas were targeted for clarification or modification: impediments to information sharing; consent and authorization procedures; parental access to minors' health information; uses and disclosures for treatment, payment, and health care operations; notices of privacy practices; minimum necessary uses and disclosures; oral communications; business associates; uses and disclosures for marketing; parents as the personal representatives of unemancipated minors; uses and disclosures for research purposes; uses and disclosures for which authorizations are required; and de-identification. On July 6, 2001 HHS

---

[8] During the 12 month period after the standards are initially adopted, the Secretary is permitted to modify the standards only if necessary to permit compliance. After the first year of adoption, HHS may modify the standards not more than once every 12 months. 42 U.S.C. § 1320d-3(b).

issued interpretative guidance materials on the rule.[9] In response to numerous and extensive comments received by HHS, along with intense lobbying efforts by various stakeholders, in March 2002 the Bush Administration issued proposed modifications to the privacy rule in the *Federal Register* at 67 Fed. Reg. 14775, and permitted a 30-day comment period on its proposal. On August 14, 2002, HHS published in the *Federal Register* the privacy rule with certain modifications, 67 Fed. Reg. 53181.[10] The August 2002 modification is virtually unchanged from the March 2002 proposal, does not require Congressional approval, and has the force of law. A summary of significant final modifications follows.

Notice

The August 2002 rule adds a new requirement for health care providers with a direct treatment relationship, that they make a good faith effort to obtain an individual's written acknowledgment of receipt of the provider's privacy notice.

Consent and Authorization

The requirement for providers to obtain an individual's prior written consent to use or disclose protected health information for treatment, payment or health care operations was eliminated. The August 2002 rule permits covered entities to obtain consent, but does not require it. Although patient authorizations will still be required to use and disclose information for purposes outside of treatment, payment, and health care operations, the August 2002 rule standardizes the core requirements in authorization forms, and allows health care groups to use a single type of authorization to get permission to use information for a specific purpose or disclosure.

Minimum Necessary

The August 2002 rule exempts from the minimum necessary standards any uses or disclosures for which an authorization has been received.

Incidental Use and Disclosure

The August 2002 rule explicitly permits incidental disclosures resulting from activities such as discussions at nursing stations, the use of sign-in sheets, calling out names in waiting rooms, etc. provided reasonable safeguards and minimum necessary requirements are met.

---

[9] Available at [http://www.hhs.gov/ocr/hipaa/finalmaster.html].
[10] Available at [http://www.hhs.gov/ocr/combinedregtext.pdf].

Business Associates

The August 2002 rule allows covered entities, except small health plans, up to one year beyond the April 14, 2003 enforcement date to change existing contracts with business associates.

Marketing

The August 2002 rule requires covered entities to obtain prior patient authorization for marketing, except for a face-to-face communication or a communication involving a promotional gift of nominal value. The rule distinguishes between activities that are and are not marketing. The definition of "marketing" in the new rules excludes communications by a health care provider promoting its own goods and services.

Medical Information of Minors

The December 2000 privacy rule generally gives control of health information about a minor to the parent, guardian, or person acting in loco parentis. The August 2002 rule clarifies that state law governs in the area of parents and minors, and that HIPAA does not overturn state laws that give providers discretion to disclose or deny health information to parents.

Research

The December 2000 privacy rule provides that protected health information may not be used or disclosed for research without either a written authorization or a waiver of authorization approved by an Institutional Review Board or a Privacy Board. In the August 2002 rule, HHS significantly simplified the administrative burdens for obtaining authorizations and assessing requests for waivers of authorization.

Disclosures to Obtain Payment

The December 2000 rule prevents a provider from disclosing protected health information to another entity for other than treatment purposes. A covered entity is permitted to disclose protected health information to other covered entities and to noncovered health care providers to enable for payment purposes.

LEGISLATION

S. 16, The Equal Rights and Equal Dignity for Americans Act, would, among other things, reverse August 2002 modifications to the privacy rule (section 903).

Chapter 5

MEDICAL RECORDS PRIVACY: QUESTIONS AND ANSWERS ON THE HIPAA FINAL RULE[†]

C. Stephen Redhead

INTRODUCTION

As of April 14, 2003, health plans and health care providers and their business associates must be in compliance with the federal health information privacy regulation. The privacy rule gives patients the right of access to their medical information and prohibits health plans and health care providers from using or disclosing individually identifiable health information without a patient's written authorization except as expressly permitted or required by the rule. For routine health care operations, including treatment and payment, plans and providers may use and disclose health information without the individual's authorization and with few restrictions. In certain other circumstances (e.g., disclosures to family members and friends), the rule requires plans and providers to give the individual the opportunity to object to the disclosure. The rule also permits the use and disclosure of health information without the individual's permission for various specified activities (e.g., public health oversight, law

---

[†] Excerpted from CRS Report RS20500. June 11, 2003.

enforcement) that are not directly connected to the treatment of the individual. For uses and disclosures that are not permitted by the regulation, plans and providers must obtain a patient's written authorization.

The privacy rule is having an important and visible impact on the administration of health care. Anyone enrolling in a health plan, picking up a prescription, or entering a doctor's office or hospital must be given a notice that describes their rights under the rule and explains how the plan or provider intends to use or disclose their health information. For their part, health plans and health care facilities must have in place reasonable administrative, technical, and physical safeguards to protect patient information from intentional or unintentional uses or disclosures that are in violation of the rule.

The health privacy rule is one of several new standards mandated by the 1996 Health Insurance Portability and Accountability Act (HIPAA) to support the growth of electronic record keeping and claims processing in the nation's health care system. The intent of the legislation is to improve the efficiency and effectiveness of health care by facilitating the electronic interchange of health information. On August 17, 2000, the Secretary of Health and Human Services (HHS) issued standards for several electronic health care transactions between plans and providers (e.g., claims for payment), including the use of uniform data codes for reporting diagnoses, referrals, authorizations, and medical procedures. The compliance deadline for the transactions and codes standards is October 16, 2003. On February 20, 2003, the Secretary published security standards to ensure the confidentiality, integrity, and availability of electronic health information. Most plans and providers have until April 21, 2005, to comply with the security standards.

The growing use of networked, electronic health information has raised serious privacy concerns among the public. Patients are increasingly worried about who has access to their medical information without their express consent. They fear that their personal health information will be used to deny them employment or insurance. HIPAA gave Congress until August 21, 1999, to enact comprehensive health privacy legislation, otherwise the HHS Secretary was instructed to develop health privacy standards. When Congress missed its self-imposed deadline, the Secretary proposed health privacy standards on November 3, 1999, and published the final rule on December 28, 2000. Modifications to the privacy rule were published on August 14, 2002.

Questions and Answers about the Health Privacy Rule

Who is Covered?

As specified under HIPAA, the privacy regulation applies to three groups of entities: (i) individual and group health plans that provide or pay for medical care; (ii) health care clearinghouses (i.e., entities that facilitate and process the flow of information between health care providers and payers); and (iii) health care providers who transmit health information electronically in a standard format in connection with one of the HIPAA-specified transactions, or who rely on third-party billing services to conduct such transactions. The rule, therefore, does not apply directly to other entities that collect and maintain health information such as life insurers, researchers, employers (unless they are acting as providers or plans), and public health officials. However, business associates with whom covered entities share health information are covered. Business associates include persons who provide legal, actuarial, accounting, data aggregation, management, administrative, accreditation, or financial services to or for a covered entity. The rule permits a covered entity to disclose health information to a business associate or to allow the business associate to create or receive health information on its behalf, provided both parties sign a written contract that essentially binds the business associate to the covered entity's privacy practices.

What Types of Health Information are Covered?

The rule covers all individually identifiable health information that is created or received by a covered entity, including genetic information and information about an individual's family history. It applies to both paper and electronic records, as well as oral communications. Nonidentifiable health data, from which all personal identifiers have been removed, are not subject to the rule.

Can Patients Access and Amend their Health Information?

Yes, covered entities must allow patients to inspect or obtain a copy of their health information, except in certain limited circumstances. Covered entities may charge a reasonable, cost-based copying fee. Patients may also request amendment or correction of information that is incorrect or incomplete. Finally, patients have the right to receive a detailed accounting of certain types of disclosures of their health information made by covered entities during the past 6 years. Disclosures for routine health care operations and those made pursuant to an authorization (see below) are exempt from the accounting requirement.

How May Plans and Providers Use and Disclose Patient Information?

The privacy rule imposes certain restrictions on when and how health plans and health care providers may use and disclose medical information. Plans and providers may use and disclose health information for treatment, payment, and other routine health care operations (TPO) without the individual's permission and with only a few restrictions. Patients have the right to request that covered entities restrict the use and disclosure of their health information for TPO, but covered entities are not required to agree to such a request.

The privacy rule also permits the disclosure of health information without a patient's authorization for various specified national priority activities, consistent with other applicable laws and regulations. First, disclosures may be made for public health purposes (e.g., reporting diseases, collecting vital statistics), as required by state and federal law. Second, health information may be disclosed to public agencies to conduct health oversight activities such as audits; inspections; civil, criminal, or administrative proceedings; and other activities necessary for oversight of the health care system. Third, disclosures may be made to law enforcement officials pursuant to a warrant, subpoena, or order issued by a judicial officer, or pursuant to a grand jury subpoena. Disclosures for law enforcement purposes are also permitted pursuant to an administrative subpoena or summons where a three-part test is met (i.e., the information is relevant, the request is specific, and non-identifiable information could not reasonably be used). Fourth, health information may be disclosed in judicial and administrative proceedings if the request for the information is made through or pursuant to a court order. Fifth, covered entities may disclose health information to researchers without a patient's authorization, provided an Institutional Review Board (IRB) or an equivalent, newly formed "privacy board" reviews the research protocol and waives the authorization requirement.[1]

---

[1] All federally funded research that involves human subjects, as well as clinical trials of new drugs and medical devices (regardless of the source of funding), are governed by a set of federal regulations called the Common Rule (45 CFR 46, Subpart A). Under the Common Rule, research proposals must be approved by an IRB, which decides whether or not to require informed consent based on the level of risk to the research subjects.

Additionally, health information may be disclosed without authorization: (i) to coroners, medical examiners, and funeral directors; (ii) to workers' compensation programs; (iii) to a government authority authorized to receive reports of abuse, neglect, or domestic violence; (iv) to organizations in order to facilitate organ, eye, and tissue donation and transplantation; (v) to government agencies for various specialized functions (e.g., national security and intelligence activities); (vi) to avert a serious threat to health or safety; (vii) and in other situations as required by law.

For the most part, the privacy rule addresses *permissible* uses and disclosures. HHS expects covered entities to rely on their professional judgement in deciding whether to permit the use or disclosure of health information covered under the rule. Covered entities are *required* to disclose information only to the individual who is the subject of the information and to HHS for enforcement of the regulation. For all uses and disclosures of health information that are not otherwise required or permitted by the rule (e.g., releasing information to financial institutions that offer mortgages and other types of loans, or selling mailing lists to marketing companies), covered entities must obtain a patient's written authorization.

Authorization forms must contain certain specified core elements including a description of the health information to be used or disclosed and the identity of the recipient of the information. In general, a covered health care provider may not condition the provision of treatment on receiving a patient's authorization. Health plans may condition enrollment or eligibility for benefits on the provision of an authorization prior to an individual's enrollment in the plan. Patients may in writing revoke their authorization at any time.

Can Medical Information be Shared with a Patient's Family or Friends?

The rule permits covered entities to disclose information to a family member, relative, close friend, or other person identified by the individual. Only information that is directly relevant to such person's involvement with the individual's care may be shared. If the individual is present and able to make health care decisions, the covered entity may disclose information if the patient has been given, in advance, the opportunity to object to any disclosures, or the covered entity reasonably infers that the patient does not object. When the patient is not present, the covered entity may use its professional judgment and experience with common practice in deciding whether a disclosure is appropriate. A pharmacist, for example, may allow a family member or other individual to pick up someone's prescription.

Does the Rule Block Access by Parents to a Minor's Information?

Generally, a parent is deemed to have the rights associated with a minor's health information, including the right to authorize disclosure or to request access to the information. However, if a minor is authorized by state law to consent to treatment and has consented to care (with or without the consent of a parent), the rule gives the minor the rights associated with that information. Whether or not a parent has access to the information is also largely governed by state law. The rule allows covered entities to disclose a minor's information to a parent if such disclosure is permitted or required by state law. Similarly, disclosure to a parent is prohibited where prohibited by state law.

Are There Limits on the Amount of Information Disclosed?

The rule requires that whenever a covered entity uses or discloses health information, or requests such information from another covered entity, it must make a reasonable effort to limit the information to the minimum amount necessary to accomplish the intended purpose of the use or disclosure. The minimum necessary standard does not apply to: treatmentrelated disclosures; disclosures made to patients upon their request; disclosures made to the Secretary to enforce compliance; any uses or disclosures for which the covered entity has received an authorization; and uses or disclosures that are required by law.

What about Incidental Disclosures?

Incidental uses and disclosures of health information that occur as a result of a use or disclosure that is otherwise permitted by the privacy regulation are not considered violations of the rule, provided that the covered entity has met the reasonable safeguards and minimum necessary standards. Examples of incidental uses and disclosures include patient sign-in sheets, bedside charts, and confidential conversations that are inadvertently overheard by others.

Are Covered Entities Required to Explain their Privacy Practices to Patients?

As noted earlier, health plans and health care providers must provide patients with a written notice of their privacy practices. Plans are required to give notice at enrollment. Providers that have a direct treatment relationship with the patient are required to give notice at the date of first service delivery and, except in emergency situations, make a good faith effort to obtain a written acknowledgment from the patient of receipt of the notice. The notice must include a description of the patient's rights, the legal duties of the covered entity, and a description of the types of uses and disclosures of information that are permitted, including those that do not require an authorization.

Does the Rule Restrict Employers' Access to Health Information?

The rule permits a group health plan to disclose individually identifiable health information to an employer that sponsors the plan, provided the information is used only for plan administration purposes. In order for a group health plan to disclose health information to a plan sponsor, the plan documents must be amended so that they limit the uses and disclosures of information by the sponsor to those consistent with the privacy rule. In addition, an employer must certify to a group health plan that it will not use the information for employment-related actions (e.g., hiring and promotion decisions). The employer must agree to establish adequate firewalls, so that only those employees that need health information to perform functions on behalf of the group health plan have access to such information.

Can Medical Information be Used for Marketing?

A covered entity may not disclose health information to a third party (e.g., pharmaceutical company), in exchange for direct or indirect remuneration, for the marketing activities of the third party without first obtaining a patient's authorization. Similarly, a covered entity may not use or disclose health information for its own marketing activities without authorization. However, communications made by a covered entity (or its business associate) to encourage a patient to purchase or use a *health care-related product or service* are not defined as marketing under the rule and, therefore, do not require the patient's authorization, even if the covered entity is paid. Such communications include prescription refill reminders and information about alternative treatments, as well as more controversial activities paid for by third parties (e.g., communications by pharmacies, paid for by a drug manufacturer, that recommend patients switch their medication to the company's product).

What Must Covered Entities do to Ensure Compliance?

Covered entities must have reasonable administrative, technical, and physical safeguards in place, commensurate with the size and scope of their business, to protect the privacy of patient information. These include designating a privacy official, training employees, and developing a system of sanctions for employees who violate the entity's policies. Covered entities are not directly liable for the actions of their business associates. They may be held liable if they know of a business associate's pattern of activity or practice in violation of the contract and they fail to take reasonable steps to correct the problem and, if such steps are unsuccessful, terminate the contract or report the problem to HHS.

Does the Rule Preempt State Health Privacy Laws?

As mandated by HIPAA, the rule does not preempt, or override, state laws that are more protective of patient privacy. Although most states do not have comprehensive health privacy laws, many states have detailed, stringent standards governing the use and disclosure of health information related to certain medical conditions, such as mental illness, genetic testing, and communicable diseases (e.g., HIV/AIDS). These stronger privacy protections will remain in force. The rule only preempts state laws that are in conflict with its requirements and that provide less stringent privacy protections. Therefore, it serves as a federal "floor" of minimum privacy protections.

How Will the Rule be Enforced?

HIPAA did not grant individuals the right to sue for violations of their health information privacy. Instead, any person who believes a covered entity is not complying with the privacy rule may file a complaint with HHS's Office of Civil Rights (OCR), which is responsible for implementing and enforcing the rule. HHS officials have said that they intend to work with covered entities to encourage voluntary compliance, and that enforcement of the rule will be reactive and complaint-driven. Under HIPAA, OCR has the authority to impose civil monetary penalties against covered entities that fail to comply with the regulation, and criminal penalties for certain wrongful disclosures of personal health information. The civil fines are $100 per incident, capped at $25,000 per year for each provision that is violated. The criminal penalties include fines of up to $250,000 and up to 10 years in prison for disclosing or obtaining health information with the intent to sell, transfer or use it for commercial advantage, personal gain, or malicious harm.

Where Can I Obtain More Information?

General information on all the HIPAA standards can be found at [http://aspe.os.dhhs.gov/admnsimp]. Answers to frequently asked questions and other details on complying with the privacy rule may be found at [http://www.hhs.gov/ocr/hipaa].

Chapter 6

COMPLIANCE WITH THE HIPAA MEDICAL PRIVACY RULE‡

Gina Marie Stevens

INTRODUCTION

As of April 14, 2003, most health care providers (including doctors and hospitals) and health plans are required to comply with the new Privacy Rule mandated by the Health Insurance Portability and Accountability Act of 1996 ("HIPAA"), and must comply with national standards to protect individually identifiable health information. The HIPAA Privacy Rule creates a federal floor of privacy protections for individually identifiable health information; establishes a set of basic consumer protections; institutes a series of regulatory permissions for uses and disclosures of protected health information; permits any person to file an administrative complaint for violations; and authorizes the imposition of civil or criminal penalties. In hearings prior to the effective date of the Rule, there was widespread concern over aspects of the rule, including the extent to which it preempted state laws. On April 17, 2003, HHS published an interim final rule establishing the rules of procedure for investigations and the imposition of civil money penalties concerning violations. This interim final rule will be effective May 19, 2003 through September 16, 2003. HHS plans to issue a complete

---

‡ Excerpted from CRS Report RS21505. April 24, 2003.

Enforcement Rule with both procedural and substantive provisions after notice-and-comment rulemaking.

BACKGROUND

In order to "improve portability and continuity of health insurance coverage in the group and individual markets,"[1] Congress enacted the Health Insurance Portability and Accountability Act of 1996 (HIPAA) on August 21, 1996, P. L. 104-191, 110 Stat. 1936, 42 U.S.C. §§ 1320d *et seq.* Subtitle F of Title II of HIPAA is entitled "Administrative Simplification," and states that the purpose of the subtitle is to improve health care by "encouraging the development of a health information system through the establishment of standards and requirements for the electronic transmission of certain health information."[2] Sections 261 through 264 of HIPAA contain the administrative simplification provisions.[3] HIPAA requires health care payers and providers who transmit transactions electronically to use standardized data elements to conduct financial and administrative transactions. Section 262 directs HHS to issue standards to facilitate the electronic exchange of information.[4] Section 263 of HIPAA delineates the duties of the National Committee on Vital and Health Statistics. Section 264 of HIPAA requires HHS to submit to the Congress detailed recommendations on standards with respect to privacy rights for individually identifiable health information. In the absence of the enactment of federal legislation, HIPAA required HHS to issue privacy regulations. The final Privacy Rule was issued by HHS and published in the *Federal Register* on December 28, 2000 at 65 Fed. Reg. 82462, shortly before the Clinton Administration left office. The Privacy Rule went into effect on April 14, 2001. On August 14, 2002, HHS published in the *Federal Register* a modified Privacy Rule, 67 Fed. Reg. 53181.[5] Enforcement of the Privacy Rule began on April 14, 2003, except for small health plans (those with annual receipts of $5 million or less) who have until April 2004 to comply.

The HIPAA Privacy Rule covers health plans, health care clearinghouses, and those health care providers who conduct certain

---

[1] H.R. Rep. No. 104-496, at 1, 66-67, reprinted in 1996 U.S.C.C.A.N. 1865, 1865-66.
[2] 110 Stat. 2021.
[3] A Brief Summary of the Medical Privacy Rule.
[4] HHS has issued final regulations on standards for security, transactions and code sets, employer identifiers, and privacy. See [http://www.hhs.gov/news/press/2002pres/hipaa.html]
[5] [http://www.hhs.gov/ocr/hipaa/finalreg.html].

financial and administrative transactions electronically.[6] Covered entities are bound by the new privacy standards even if they contract with others (called "business associates") to perform essential functions. HIPAA does not give HHS authority to regulate other private businesses or public agencies. Covered entities that fail to comply with the rule are subject to civil and criminal penalties,[7] but individuals do not have the right to sue for violations of the rule. Instead, the law provides that individuals must direct their complaints to HHS' Office for Civil Rights (OCR).[8] OCR maintains a Web site with information on the new regulation, including guidance at [http://www.hhs.gov/ocr/hipaa/]. HHS also recently issued a 20 page "Summary of the HIPAA Privacy Rule."[9] HHS will enforce the civil money penalties, and the Department of Justice will enforce the criminal penalties. Criminal penalties may be imposed if the offense is committed under false pretenses, with intent to sell the information or reap other personal gain.

HIPAA authorizes the HHS Secretary to impose civil money penalties of up to $25,000 for each year for those entities failing to comply with the privacy rule.[10] Several statutory limitations are imposed on the Secretary's authority to impose civil money penalties (CMP). A penalty may not be imposed: with respect to an act that constitutes an offense punishable under the criminal penalty provision; "if it is established to the satisfaction of the Secretary that the person liable for the penalty did not know, and by exercising reasonable diligence would not have known, that such person violated the provisions;"[11] if "the failure to comply was due to reasonable cause and not to willful neglect" and is corrected within a certain time period.[12] A CMP may be reduced or waived "to the extent that the payment of such penalty would be excessive relative to the compliance failure involved."[13] In addition, a number of procedural requirements are incorporated by reference in HIPAA that are relevant to the imposition of CMP's.[14] The Secretary may not initiate a CMP action "later than six months after the date" of the occurrence that forms the basis for the CMP action. The Secretary may initiate a CMP by serving notice in a manner authorized by Rule 4 of the Federal Rules of Civil Procedure. The Secretary must give

---

[6] For information on covered entities, see [http://www.cms.gov/hipaa/hipaa2/support/tools/decisionsupport/default.asp].
[7] 65 Fed. Reg. 82,462, 82,487 (Dec. 28, 2000); see [http://www.hhs.gov/ocr/hipaa/finalreg.html]
[8] See [http://www.ehcca.com/presentations/hipaa6/campanelli.pdf].
[9] [http://www.hhs.gov/ocr/privacysummary.pdf].
[10] 42 U.S.C. § 1320d-5(a)(1).
[11] 42 U.S.C. § 1320d-5(b)(2).
[12] 42 U.S.C. § 1320d-5(b)(3).
[13] 42 U.S.C. § 1320d-5(b)(4).
[14] 42 U.S.C. § 1320d-5(a)(2).

written notice to the person to whom he wishes to impose a CMP and an opportunity for a determination to made "on the record after a hearing at which the person is entitled to be represented by counsel, to present witnesses, and to cross-examine witnesses against the person."[15] Judicial review of the Secretary's determination and the issuance and enforcement of subpoenas is available in the United States Court of Appeals.

With respect to ascertaining compliance with and enforcement of the Privacy Rule, the Secretary of HHS is to seek the voluntary cooperation of covered entities. The Secretary is authorized to provide technical assistance to covered entities in order to facilitate their voluntary compliance. Enforcement and other activities to facilitate compliance include the provision of technical assistance; responding to questions; providing interpretations and guidance; responding to state requests for preemption determinations; investigating complaints and conducting compliance reviews; and seeking civil monetary penalties and making referrals for criminal prosecution.

An individual may file a compliant with the Secretary if the individual believes that the covered entity is not complying with the rule.[16] Complaints must be filed in writing, either on paper or electronically; name the entity that is the subject of the complaint and describe the acts or omissions believed to be in violation of the applicable requirements of the Privacy Rule; and be filed within 180 days of when the complainant knew or should have known that the act or omission complained of occurred, unless the time limit is waived by the Secretary for good cause shown. Complaints to the Secretary may be filed only with respect to alleged violations occurring on or after April 14, 2003. The Secretary has delegated to the Office for Civil Rights (OCR) the authority to receive and investigate complaints as they may relate to the Privacy Rule.[17] Individuals may file written complaints with OCR by mail, fax or e-mail. For information about the Privacy Rule or the process for filing a complaint with OCR, they may contact any OCR office or go to [http://www.hhs.gov/ocr/howtofileprivacy.htm]. After April 14, 2003, individuals have a right to file a complaint directly with the covered entity, and are directed to refer to the covered entity's notice of privacy practices for information about how to file a complaint.

The Secretary's investigation may include a review of the policies, procedures, or practices of the covered entity, and of the circumstances regarding the alleged acts or omissions. The Secretary is also authorized to

---

[15] 42 U.S.C. § 1320a-7a(c)(2).
[16] 45 CFR section 160.306.
[17] 65 Fed. Reg. At 82,474, 82,487.

conduct compliance reviews. Covered entities are required to provide records and compliance reports to the Secretary to determine compliance; and to cooperate with complaint investigations and compliance reviews. In cases where an investigation or compliance review has indicated noncompliance, the Secretary is to inform the covered entity and the complainant in writing, and attempt to resolve the matter informally. If the Secretary determines that the matter cannot be resolved informally, the Secretary may issue written findings documenting the noncompliance. In cases where no violation is found, the Secretary is to inform the covered entity and the complainant in writing.

On April 17, 2003 HHS published an interim final "Enforcement Rule" that applies to standards, including the Privacy Rule, adopted under the Administrative Simplification provisions of HIPAA, 68 *Fed. Reg.* 18895.[18] The interim final rule establishes procedures for investigations, imposition of penalties, and hearings for civil money penalties; and is effective May 19, 2003 thru September 16, 2003. It is to be revised when HHS issues a complete Enforcement rule that will include procedural **and** substantive requirements for the imposition of civil money penalties, such as HHS' policies for determining violations and calculating CMP's. Although HHS recognized that the Administrative Procedure Act (APA) requires that most of the provisions of the complete Enforcement Rule be promulgated through notice-and-comment rulemaking, it concluded that the interim final rule's procedural provisions are exempted from the requirement for notice and comment rulemaking under the "rules of agency . . . procedure, or practice" exemption of the APA, 5 U.S.C. § 553(b)(3)(A). As a result, HHS published the procedural rules in final form without notice-and-comment to inform covered entities and the public of the procedural requirements for compliance. In addition, HHS requests public comment thru June 16, 2003 on the interim final rule.

The National Committee on Vital and Health Statistics (NCVHS) serves as the statutory public advisory body to the Secretary of Health and Human Services in the area of health data and statistics.[19] As part of its responsibilities under the Health Insurance Portability and Accountability Act of 1996 (HIPAA), the National Committee on Vital and Health Statistics (NCVHS) monitors the implementation of the Administrative Simplification

---

[18] Department of Health and Human Services, Civil Money Penalties: Procedures for Investigations, Imposition of Penalties, and Hearings, 68 Fed. Reg. 18895 (Apr. 17, 2003), at [http://a257.g.akamaitech.net/7/257/2422/14mar20010800/edocket.access.gpo.gov/2003/pdf/0 3-9497.pdf].

[19] 42 U.S.C. 242k(k).

provisions of HIPAA, including the Standards for Privacy of Individually Identifiable Health Information (Privacy Rule). Last fall, the NCVHS held three hearings to learn about the implementation activities of covered entities. In its November 2002 letter to Secretary Thompson summarizing its findings the Committee stated that "there is an extremely high level of confusion, misunderstanding, frustration, anxiety, fear, and anger as the April 14, 2003 compliance date nears."[20] Reportedly the Privacy Rule has "touched off a quiet revolution in the health care industry."[21] According to NCVHS, the OCR is widely viewed as not providing adequate guidance and technical assistance as evidenced by the lack of model notices of privacy practices, acknowledgments, authorizations, and other forms. The general guidance was judged to be of limited value because of special industry or professional circumstances, and NCVHS reported that witnesses conveyed a great sense of frustration that they could not obtain clarification from OCR or answers to the questions they submitted. Covered entities report the undertaking of substantial compliance measures ranging from the adoption of new policies, the training of employees, and the development of privacy notices.

Another area of widespread concern at the NCVHS hearings was HIPAA preemption. According to NCVHS, witnesses said that issues of preemption made compliance much more difficult, costly, and complicated. The term "preemption" is a judicial doctrine that originated through interpretation of the Supremacy Clause of the United States Constitution.[22] In effect, the Supremacy Clause stands for the proposition that the Constitution and the laws of the federal government rise above the laws of the states. As a result, federal law will always override state law in cases of conflict. Absent a direct conflict, however, preemption depends on the intent of Congress. Such intent may be express or implied. Express preemption exists when Congress explicitly commands that a state law be displaced. Where Congress has not expressly preempted state and local laws, two types of implied federal preemption may be found: field preemption, in which federal regulation is so pervasive that one can reasonably infer that states or

---

[20] [http://ncvhs.hhs.gov/021125lt.htm].
[21] Robert Pear, *Health System Wearily Prepares for Privacy Rule*, N.Y. TIMES, Apr. 6, 2003; [http://query.nytimes.com/gst/abstract.html?res=F40C13FD395C0C758CDDAD0894DB404 482]
[22] The Supremacy Clause provides: "This Constitution, and the Laws of the United States which shall be made in Pursuance thereof; and all Treaties made, or which shall be made, under the Authority of the United States, shall be the supreme Law of the Land; and the Judges in every State shall be bound thereby, any Thing in the Constitution or Laws of any state to the Contrary notwithstanding." U.S.Const. art. VI, cl. 2.

localities have no role to play, and conflict preemption, in which "compliance with both federal and state regulations is a physical impossibility, or where the state law "stands as an obstacle to the accomplishment and execution of the full purposes and objectives of Congress."[23]

HIPAA sets forth a general rule, based on the principles of conflict preemption. Basically, this rule establishes that any federal regulation resulting from implementation of the Act preempts any contrary state law.[24] "Contrary" is defined as situations where: (1) a covered entity would find it impossible to comply with both the state and the federal requirements, or (2) when the state law stands as an obstacle to the accomplishment and execution of the full purposes and objectives of Congress.[25] Congress established three exceptions to this general rule. First, there is an exception for state laws that the Secretary determines are necessary to prevent fraud and abuse, to ensure appropriate state regulation of insurance and health plans, for state reporting on health care delivery, or for other purposes.[26] The second exception provides that state laws will not be superseded if the Secretary determines that the law addresses controlled substances.[27] Both of these exceptions require an affirmative "exception determination" from the Secretary of HHS for the state law not to be preempted.[28] The third exception provides that state laws will not be preempted if they relate to the privacy of individually identifiable health information and are "more stringent" than the federal requirements.[29] A state law is "more stringent" if it meets one or more of the following criteria: 1) the state law prohibits or further limits the use or disclosure of protected health information, except if the disclosure is required by HHS to determine a covered entity's compliance or is to the individual who is the subject of the individually identifiable information; 2) the state law permits individuals with greater rights of access to or amendment of their individually identifiable health information; provided, however, HIPAA will not preempt a state law to the extent that it authorizes or prohibits disclosure of protected health information about a minor to a parent, guardian or person acting in loco parentis of such minor; 3) the state law provides for more information to be disseminated to the

---

[23] *Gade v. National Solid Wastes Mgmt. Assn.*, 505 U.S. 88, 98 (1992).
[24] 42 U.S.C. § 1320d-7(a)(1).
[25] 45 C.F.R. 160.202.
[26] 42 U.S.C. § 1320d-7(a)(2)(A)(i).
[27] 42 U.S.C. § 1320d-7(a)(2)(A)(ii).
[28] See 45 C.F.R. 160.203(a), 160.204.
[29] 42 U.S.C. § 1320d-7(a)(2)(B) in conjunction with 42 U.S.C. 1320d-2 note (Section 264(c)(2) of Public Law 104-191).

individual regarding use and disclosure of their protected health information and rights and remedies; 4) the state law narrows the scope or duration of authorization or consent, increases the privacy protections surrounding authorization and consent, or reduces the coercive effect of the surrounding circumstances; 5) the state law imposes stricter standards for record keeping or accounting of disclosures; 6) the state law strengthens privacy protections for individuals with respect to any other matter.[30]

In addition to the general rule and exceptions, Congress "carved out" two provisions whereby certain areas of state authority will not be limited or invalidated by HIPAA rules. First, the public health "carve out" saves any law providing for the reporting of disease or injury, child abuse, birth, or death for the conduct of public surveillance, investigation or intervention.[31] The second "carve out" allows states to regulate health plans by requiring the plans to report, or provide access to, information for the purpose of audits, program monitoring and evaluation, or the licensure or certification.[32]

LEGISLATION

S. 16, The Equal Rights and Equal Dignity for Americans Act of 2003, would, in section 903, reverse the August 2002 modifications to the privacy rule.

---

[30] See 45 C.F.R. 160.202.
[31] 42 U.S.C. 1320d-7(b).
[32] 42 U.S.C. 1320d-7(c).

INDEX

A

Accredited Standards Committee (ASC), 64, 84
Acquired Immune Deficiency Syndrome (AIDS), 16, 40, 81, 108
activities of daily living (ADLs), 50
administrative costs, vii, 2-4, 12, 53, 68, 86
Administrative Procedure Act (APA), 113
alcohol, 61
American Hospital Association (AHA), 76, 83, 85
American Medical Association (AMA), 75-77, 85
American National Standards Institute (ANSI), 4, 64
anxiety, 114
Association of American Medical Colleges (AAMC), 80, 85
automated teller machines (ATMs), 71

B

Blue Cross Blue Shield (BCBS), 32, 82, 83, 85

C

California, 31, 61
cancer, 23, 38, 81
civil mone(tar)y penalties (CMP), viii, 42, 88, 90, 96, 97, 108, 109, 111-113
clinical trials, 80, 104
COBRA premiums, 46
Common Rule, 80, 104
communicable disease(s), 81, 108
Consolidated Appropriations Act, 67
Consolidated Omnibus Budget Reconciliation Act (COBRA), vii, 25, 28, 34, 43, 46
consumer protection, 41, 50, 51, 91, 109
controlled substances, 8, 90, 115
coroners, 90, 96, 105
cost-effectiveness, 80
covered entities, 47, 73-81, 83, 84, 88-90, 95, 96, 98, 99, 103-106, 108, 111-114
criminal penalty provision, 111
criminal prosecution, 16, 112

D

data codes, 53, 102

death, 8, 34, 51, 116
Department of Health and Human Services (DHHS), viii, 4, 42, 91, 113
Department of Justice, 97, 111
Designated Standards Maintenance Organizations (DSMOs), 64
detailed records, 56
diagnostic tests, 2, 56, 65
digital records, 57
discrimination, 15, 20, 45, 61
domestic violence, 35, 90, 96, 105
donation, 90, 105

E

education, 73
electronic data interchange (EDI), vii, 53, 55, 57, 65
eligibility, 2, 5, 22, 25, 28, 29, 34, 35, 43, 55, 56, 63, 86, 90, 105
Employee Retirement Income Security Act (ERISA), 20, 29, 38, 40, 42
Employer Identification Number (EIN), 67
employers, 2, 4-6, 10, 12, 13, 19, 20, 22, 24, 26, 37-40, 43, 45, 47, 54, 56, 61, 63, 67, 68, 72, 78, 81, 86, 91, 93, 103
employer-sponsored plans, 39, 64
ERISA amendments, 20

F

Federal Employee's Health Benefits Plans (FEHBP), 28, 41
federal law(s), 11, 15-17, 61, 93, 104, 114
Federal Register, 6, 26, 29, 37, 63, 66, 67, 69, 72, 74, 84, 94, 98, 110
federal regulation, 16, 80, 104, 114, 115
federal requirements, 19, 40, 115

federal standards, 9, 19, 39
federally directed registry, 66
federally funded research, 80
fee-for-service, 55, 56
final rule, viii, 6, 13, 47, 54, 63, 64, 66, 67, 69, 72, 76, 78, 82, 83, 102, 109, 113
financial risk, 48, 56
funding, 80, 104
funeral directors, 90, 105

G

General Accounting Office (GAO), 21, 37, 85, 97
genetic information, 15, 23, 35, 103
Gore, Vice President, 67
government authority, 105
group health plan, 4, 20, 22-24, 26, 27, 29, 34-36, 38, 39, 41, 42, 44-46, 103, 107
group market, 28, 31, 37, 44

H

Health and Human Services (HHS), vii, viii, 4-6, 9-13, 21, 37, 42, 47, 51, 53-56, 63, 64, 66-70, 72-76, 78, 79, 82-85, 88, 90, 91, 94, 96, 97, 99, 102, 105, 108-113, 115
health care delivery, 2, 8, 12, 55, 57, 87, 115
Health Care Financing Administration (HCFA), 6, 44, 45, 65, 66, 87, 88
Health Care Financing Administration Procedure Coding System (HCPCS), 65, 66, 84
health care fraud, 95
health care providers, viii, 4-6, 10, 12, 13, 15, 54-56, 63, 64, 66, 72, 75, 79, 82, 86, 88, 95, 98, 99, 101, 103, 104, 106, 109, 110
health care quality, 61

Index

health care services, 1, 2, 4, 8, 65, 77
health care, vii, viii, 1-6, 8, 10-16, 23, 35, 36, 38, 39, 46-48, 50, 53-57, 59, 61, 63-69, 71-83, 86-95, 97-99, 101-107, 109, 110, 114, 115
health industry, 17, 68
health information, viii, 2-5, 7, 9-12, 14-17, 21, 47, 54-57, 59-62, 67, 69, 72-76, 78-82, 86-90, 92, 94-99, 101-110, 115
Health Insurance Reforms, 22, 40
health insurance, vii, 2, 4, 15, 19-34, 37-39, 42-45, 47-50, 52, 55-57, 61, 68, 76, 87, 93, 110
health maintenance organization(s) (HMO(s)), 4, 19, 20, 37, 40, 42, 52, 74, 77
health privacy protections, 67
health services, 2, 4, 9, 21, 38, 56, 80
high risk activities, 40
home health agencies, 79
hospitals, viii, 2, 12, 56, 65, 68, 74, 76, 79, 80, 93, 109
housing, 47, 60

I

individual patients, 56
individual retirement account (IRA), 52
information security, viii, 54, 57, 59, 60, 69, 71
Institutional Review Board (IRB), 80, 99, 104
insurers, 2, 3, 10, 12, 15, 19, 30, 37, 38, 39, 42, 43, 56, 65, 68, 72-74, 76, 77, 79, 93, 103
integrated information, 68
Internal Revenue Code (IRC), 20, 39, 42
Internal Revenue Service (IRS), 42, 44, 45, 48, 67
intervention(s), 8, 10, 56, 82, 116
interventions

J

Joint Commission for the Accreditation of Healthcare Organizations (JCAHO), 79

K

knowledge, 60, 78

L

lawmakers, 39, 61, 62
level of disability, 50
liability, 78, 80, 97
limits on coverage, 39
long-term care, 4, 20, 49-51

M

managed (health) care, 2, 3, 12, 15, 55, 56, 68
managed care organizations (MCOs), 56
media, 68
medicaid programs, 7, 65, 66
Medicaid, 2, 4, 7, 23, 28, 29, 56, 65, 84
medical examiners, 90, 96, 105
medical expenses, 20, 35, 48, 49, 52
medical history, 35, 37, 55, 63
medical records privacy, viii, 14, 15, 16, 54, 93
Medical Savings Account(s) (MSA(s)), 19, 20, 46, 48, 93
medical schools, 80
medical services, 40, 56, 65
Medicare, 2, 4, 7, 23, 28, 29, 50, 51, 56
mental health coverage, 38, 39
Mental Health Parity Act (MHPA), 38, 39, 44
mental health, 3, 16, 21, 27, 38, 39, 44, 97

model, 26, 83, 114

N

National Association of Insurance Commissioners (NAIC), 30, 51, 52
National Committee on Vital and Health Statistics (NCVHS), 4, 9, 12, 68, 69, 84, 86, 87, 110, 113, 114
National Council for Prescription Drug Programs (NCDCP), 4, 64, 84
National Drug Codes (NDC), 65
National Employer Identifier, 67
National Information Assurance Partnership (NIAP), 72
National Institute of Standards and Technology (NIST), 71, 72
National Medicaid EDI HIPAA (NMEH), 65
National Provider System (NPS), 66
Newborns' and Mothers' Health Protection Act, 39, 45
Notice of Proposed Rulemaking (NPRM), 67, 88
nursing homes, 79

O

Office for Civil Rights (OCR), 96, 108, 111, 112, 114

P

parents, 82, 97, 99
participating providers, 56
Pension Welfare Benefits Administration (PWBA), 44, 45
pharmacies, 12, 68, 107
pharmacist(s), 76, 78, 105
PHS Act, 20
physicians, 2, 12, 55-57, 64, 68, 76-79, 93

portability and renewability standards, 42
prescription drugs, 27, 65
Privacy Board (PB), 80, 99
privacy rule, viii, 47, 54, 63, 68, 69, 72-75, 79, 80, 82-85, 91, 93, 95, 97, 99-102, 104, 105, 107, 108, 111, 116
privacy standards, viii, 9, 47, 54, 87, 102, 111
private sector, 93
Public Health Service (PHS), 9, 20, 38, 45, 87

Q

quality assessment, 56, 76
quality of health care, 2, 55, 56, 68

R

restrictions, 15, 19, 27, 29, 36, 40-42, 48, 73-75, 89, 90, 93, 95, 101, 104

S

safeguards, 5, 15, 16, 47, 57, 86, 92, 98, 102, 106, 107
self-employed, 19, 20, 21, 48, 49
self-insured employers, 38
service delivery, 106
services, 55-57, 65, 70, 73, 75, 76, 78, 79, 89, 90, 99, 103
Social Security Act, 3, 7, 13, 46, 86
social security, 67, 68
standards development organizations (SDOs), 64
Standards for the Privacy of Individually Identifiable Health Information, viii, 91
state law(s), viii, 7-9, 11, 15-17, 21, 29, 37, 40-43, 52, 81-83, 87, 90, 93, 96, 97, 99, 106, 108, 109, 114, 115

state regulation, 30, 38, 115
substance abuse, 27, 97
surgery, 21, 38, 76

T

teaching hospitals, 80
tests, 2, 56, 65
training, 80, 90, 107, 114
transplantation, 90, 105
treatment limitations, 38, 39
treatment, 2, 20, 23, 27, 38-40, 44, 49, 50, 52, 55, 56, 61, 73-79, 81, 89, 90, 92, 93, 95-99, 101, 104-106

treatment, payment, and other routine health care operations (TPO), 104

U

uniform standards, 71
unique individual identifier, 12, 17, 67, 68
utilization review, 56

W

workers' compensation programs, 90, 105